RACING CARS

Doug Nye

NEW YORK

Author	**Doug Nye**
Illustrators	**Hayward Art Group Linda Rogers Associates**
	Tom Brittain
Editor	**Tim Auger**
Designer	**Ron Pickless**
Consultant	**Michael Ware**

First published in USA 1981
by Exeter Books

Distributed by Bookthrift, Inc
New York, New York

Designed and produced by
Grisewood and Dempsey Limited
141-143 Drury Lane, London WC2
© Grisewood and Dempsey Limited 1980

Color separations by Newsele Litho Ltd, Milan
Printed and bound by South China Printing Co, Hong Kong

ISBN 0-89673-069-7

Contents

Introduction

What is a racing car? For the purpose of this volume it is not merely a car which is raced occasionally, but one which has been built specifically for competition purposes. There are a few exceptions, such as the 1890s Panhard, and the 1903 Gordon Bennett-winning Mercedes '60', which to some extent doubled as road-going non-competition designs. Most of them won the 'classic' tag by success in competition; some others were notably unsuccessful in racing but deserve mention for technical innovation or sophistication.

It was in 1894 that the first properly organized motoring competition took place, in France, in the form, virtually, of a rally. Then, in 1895, motor racing got under way.

The first true motor race in the modern sense was run on May 29, 1895 in northern Italy, from Turin to the village of Asti and back. It attracted only five contestants: a Benz car, a four-seat Daimler omnibus, a steamer christened *Staffetta* and two Hildebrand-und-Wolfmüller motor-cycles. The steamer broke down, the Benz driver abandoned all hope at Asti and Simone Federmann in the Daimler won at 9.6 mph from the two motor-cyclists. The world, or that tiny part of it which heard of the event, evidently grunted and turned over the page for some interesting news . . .

Twelve days later the age of racing began in France, in spectacular style. The newly formed Automobile Club de France had organized a race over no less than 745 miles, from Paris to Bordeaux and back. The Club received 97 entries, which yielded 22 actual starters and 9 road-weary finishers. First home, almost six hours clear of the second-place man, was Emile Levassor, at the tiller of one of his own 4 hp twin-cylinder Daimler-engined Panhard-et-Levassors. Levassor drove the whole distance single-handed, and, apart from brief halts at controls, non-stop. He had reached his anticipated crew changeover point three hours early; his relief driver and mechanic had not yet appeared there but he would not wait. Nor would he hand over the tiller to his own riding mechanic, and clattered on through the night by the dull glimmer of his oil-burning carriage lamp. After a stop at Bordeaux lasting only four minutes, Levassor turned about and charged through another night. He fell asleep once, hitting a bank without doing any severe damage to his steed, and 48 hours 48 minutes after leaving Paris he returned there to the Finish line—having averaged a remarkable 15.07 mph. By the race rules first place was awarded to the first four-seater car, and Levassor's special two-seater was denied victory, but there was no doubt of his heroic reception by the French public.

Thereafter, the development of motor-racing and the cars themselves was explosive. Engines grew larger and larger as designers sought more power and therefore speed, virtually regardless of weight. Company promoters and publicists saw the new sport as an instant way of selling their wares. The buying public neither knew nor cared that the latest racing Panhard, De Dietrich or Mors bore little resemblance to the car they would buy. Racing success, then as now, proved that the manufacturer knew what he was doing.

Slowly the character of racing changed, as the city-to-city era was ended by accidents. Circuit racing took over, usually on public roads closed for the occasion. The first Grand Prix, in 1906, was run on a 64-mile circuit, while laps above 50 miles were commonplace. These circuits had to be covered up to a dozen times to create a worthy test of speed and endurance.

From 1900 to 1905 the pre-Grand Prix international competition for the Gordon Bennett Trophy concentrated (largely unwarranted) attention upon strictly prescribed three-car teams from each interested manufacturing country. Cars changed during this period from early primitives with 5-litre 25 bhp engines to 10–16-litre models developing as much as 90–120 bhp at 1000–1400 rpm.

The Gordon Bennett competition's regulations took no account of the relative strengths of different national motor industries. The French became heartily tired of this, and founded their Grand Prix race in 1906. This was a one-off annual event. It was not until after World War I that other national Grand Prix races began to join the French Grand Prix to form the annual series of up to 17 World Championship Grandes Epreuves which we see today. There was a very low-key World Championship run by the governing body of the sport, the AIACR, in 1924–25 but it was not a competition which sparked the public's imagination until re-introduced in 1950 as the Drivers' World Championship.

But this was far in the future. When Grand Prix racing began, cars were derived from Gordon Bennett models with four-cylinder short-stroke engines of 12–18 litres capacity developing over 100 bhp. The riding mechanic was a very vital member of the crew in those days. The driver had his work cut out fighting to aim his car over the loose-surfaced roadways of the time, and controlling the throttle and brakes; his mechanic was constantly at work maintaining air-pressure in the fuel tank (to force fuel through to the engine) and monitoring oil drip-feed to lubricate that hardworking engine.

In 1908 there was wider use of dropped frames curving down between front and rear axles to lower the overall height, and scuttles began to be built up to afford driver and mechanic greater protection from the elements.

Grand Prix racing was abandoned from 1909 to 1911 in response partly to a trade recession, but largely to Germany's defeat of the French establishment in the 1908 race. Voiturette racing – effectively the 'Formula 2' of the time – took precedence and new marques came to prominence, such as Peugeot and Delage. When the Grand Prix was revived in 1912 using tarred road surfaces for the first time, there was a titanic struggle between the new voiturette-derived lightweight cars and the old chain-drive, big-engined monsters as exemplified by Fiat. With their 7.6-litre cars Peugeot initiated the trend towards more modest engines in lighter chassis made fast

Théry changing tyres on his Brasier at the Col de la Moréno depot during the 1905 Gordon Bennett race around the Auvergne, France.

by technical sophistication, while the voiturette race run concurrently showed the form of things to come with a flock of refined three-litre cars.

Peugeot dominated the racing season of 1913—as related in detail in later pages—and such Brooklands track-derived British trickery as streamlined wind-cheating tails was expressly forbidden by the French club's regulations.

By 1914 the Peugeot-inspired practice of using four valves per cylinder actuated by twin overhead camshafts had become generally accepted, and engine output at the new 4.5-litre limit averaged 120 bhp at 2800 rpm in cars weighing about 1.2 tons. Seat height was lowered by the use of double-drop-frame side rails and Peugeot learned the Brooklands Brooklands lesson—fitting tapering-tail bodies. During the Great War years racing was confined to the USA where 1914 Grand Prix cars like the Mercédès and Peugeot were widely successful in track racing. In 1919 the post-war straight-eight-engined Ballot cars achieved superior lap speeds despite their traditional bolster-tank bodywork in place of the fashionable tapering tail-cones, but this regression proved to be temporary.

In 1920 in Europe long tails in the American Indianapolis track-racing style became generally accepted, and when the Grand Prix was revived in 1921 based on three-litre US regulations, there was almost universal use of long-stroke straight-eight-cylinder engines with more than two valves per cylinder, giving 115–120 bhp at 3500–4200 rpm. Long-tailed bodies with staggered seating were widely used, the riding mechanic being tucked behind and to one side of his driver, often with a cut-out tail cowl into which he could fit his arm, embracing the driver's back.

When a new two-litre limit was applied for Grand Prix racing in the years 1922–25, four- and six-cylinder engines were revived, developing 80–90 bhp at 4500–5000 rpm in small cars weighing about three quarters of a ton. Road surfaces were much improved during this period and the mass start became general, superseding a staggered start for each car at 30-second intervals.

By 1925 the riding mechanic had been banned. He was thought to be vulnerable in the event of an accident, and no longer necessary, since tyre changing and mechanical repairs on shorter circuits could usually be done in the service pits. Driving-mirrors therefore became obligatory. The French Grand Prix was run for the first time on an artificial road circuit, the 7.6-mile course at

A 1932 Alfa Romeo P3 'Tipo B' Monoposto being raced in a VSCC event by its owner, Bill Summers.

the Montlhéry Autodrome. This was also the first Sunday Grand Prix.

New 1.5-litre regulations were applied in 1926, and manufacturers adopted straight-eight engines with roller bearings, offset to the left-side of the car. The offset driver's seat was mounted down alongside the propeller-shaft, which now passed through the position previously occupied by the mechanic. A very low driving position was thus achieved. Bugatti were very successful with a more traditional car, but in 1927 their dual-purpose true two-seater-type car was out-classed as the new purpose-built Grand Prix models achieved full development.

From 1928 to 1930 there was general disregard of regulations as money was short, and two-litre models from 1922 to 1925 regained popularity. There was widespread use of two-seater bodies to make cars usable in both Grand Prix and sports car form. In the years 1930 to 1933 Formule Libre (Free Formula) became accepted without restriction on size of engine or car. Works-sponsored teams and drivers reappeared to oust the amateur enthusiasts once again, and largely unsuccessful experiments were made with engines of between four and five litres capacity developing up to 300 bhp. What was decisively successful was the introduction of single central seats placed above the propeller-shaft in slim-line bodies, reminiscent of the type used in US track events during the twenties. The definitive form of single-seater racing car had evolved.

In 1934 the new 750 kg maximum-weight Formula saw the German state-backed teams of Mercedes-Benz and Auto Union developing sledge-hammers to crack the Grand Prix nut.

Giuseppe Campari winning the 1924 French Grand Prix at Lyon in his works Alfa Romeo P2.

All Grand Prix cars except Bugatti now featured a centrally located single seat, and all, with the exception of Auto Union, adopted straight-eight engines.

During the unlimited-capacity years up to 1937 Mercedes-Benz perfected the most powerful Grand Prix engine ever seen, delivering 646 bhp on the test-bed and around 600 bhp in the chassis. In 1980, 43 years later, the best-developed Formula 1 three-litre engines were capable of a genuine 500 bhp and the near-perfected 1.5-litre turbocharged Renault V6 ran nearer 550 bhp on occasion.

This titanic Formula ran into 1937 and was replaced by a new and restrictive class demanding a minimum – as opposed to the former maximum – weight limit of 850 kg for cars of only three litres supercharged or 4.5 litres unsupercharged. Central-single-seater bodyshells were mounted on chassis powered by complex V12-cylinder engines developing 400–450 bhp.

Meanwhile voiturette racing had continued alongside the Grand Prix classes, with the 1.5-litre supercharged class of the thirties dominated by ERA, Maserati and finally Alfa Romeo, with one brief intrusion by Mercedes-Benz. There were other popular classes too, for 750 cc and 1100 cc racing cars, but there is insufficient space in these pages to cover examples of these cars which were in any case derived largely from Grand Prix and 1.5-litre Voiturette practice.

World War II was to put a temporary end to motor racing. In Europe, still the centre of road-racing competition, the full stop came in 1940, while in American track racing, the calendar ran uninterrupted through the season of 1941. On both sides of the Atlantic, racing recommenced in 1946, despite shattered road communications around Europe, and extreme shortages of fuel, tyres and even sparking plugs. The pre-war Italian voiturettes were a dominant force in Europe; only Alfa Romeo entered a true works team, and succeeded accordingly.

The three years 1947 to 1949 saw competition between what had been the pre-war 1500 cc Voiturette class and the 4.5-litre unsupercharged pre-war division of Grand Prix models, and this proved a far fairer match than the three-litre supercharged class raced so expensively by the German teams of 1938–39.

In 1950–51 a successful challenge to the dominance of supercharged racing engines was mounted by Ferrari with a complex 4.5-litre unsupercharged V12 engine of modern design. With over 350 bhp in chassis weighing less than one ton, Ferrari eventually toppled Alfa Romeo, and when the great Milan factory team retired at the end of the 1951 season there was no realistic competition left to face Ferrari. Consequently in 1952–53 Grand Prix World Championship events were thrown open to two-litre unsupercharged Formula 2 cars, this Formula having grown in recent years along with the British-developed 500 cc motor-cycle-engined Formula 3, now recognized internationally.

The first true postwar Grand Prix Formula was established in the period 1954–60 with an allowance of 2.5 litres unsupercharged and only 750 cc supercharged – a comparison which finally killed off the supercharged racing engine for a quarter-century. While the 'Two-and-a-halves' contested Grands Prix racing using alcohol-based fuels and running 300-mile distances through 1957, a new 1.5-litre Formula 2 was developed which was to bring to the fore smaller manufacturers who specialized in building only racing cars – teams like Cooper and Lotus in Britain. A factor in the trend towards specialist racing-car constructors, using engines and gearboxes from outside proprietary sources, was the concentration on personality rather than marque resulting from the introduction in 1950 of the Drivers' World Championship. This offended some of the manufacturers involved, and some mass-production companies who also built racing cars drifted away towards rallying and other promotional activities.

When the 1958 regulation changes were

made, which allowed Grand Prix distances to be reduced to 300 km or two hours minimum, and also banned the use of alcohol fuels in favour of straight aviation petrol, the small British teams with their supply of proprietary engines from Coventry Climax began to come to the fore. Their small lightweight chassis far outperformed the tradition-steeped frames from Continental manufacturers such as Ferrari and Maserati, and in particular Cooper's rear-engined – or more properly 'mid-engined' – layout signposted the way ahead. By 1960 all worthwhile Grand Prix teams and many involved in the minor Formulae had their engine behind the driver's cockpit and Lotus in particular broke new ground with sophisticated suspension systems and high-quality chassis forms which are still with us today.

In 1961–65, what had been the 1.5-litre Formula 2 was elevated to Formula 1 Grand Prix status with a few extra safety regulations added, and then in 1966 the return of power was heralded by the adoption of a new three-litre unsupercharged Formula. This has come to be dominated by Cosworth-Ford with their DFV V8 three-litre engine, and more recently by Ferrari's powerful flat-12 312 unit from Italy. But in 1977 Renault returned to Grand Prix racing with the first engine of the current Formula to make use of the 1.5-litre super-charged option, in this case with an exhaust-driven turbo-supercharger. In the French Grand Prix of 1979, the French nationalized *Régie* scored the first forced-induction Grande-Epreuve win since Fangio's Alfa Romeo 159 won at Barcelona in 1951.

In the pages which follow some of the out-standing cars of motor-racing's long and varied history are covered in some detail. They trace essentially the story of Grand Prix racing with occasional diversions into minor Formulae and American track racing on the relatively few occasions when these have reversed the trend of technical development and have fed something back into the Grand Prix mainstream. The arrangement is basically chronological, with the cars in each year placed alphabetically, although there are one or two departures from that rule where it makes sense to group particular cars together, or where a particularly important car merits a two-page spread to itself. I have sought to describe within the space available the back-ground to each car's design and development, and its significance in the overall scheme of things; there is also some reference to the personalities who drove them, and to those who worked on design and development. On occasion the selection of one car rather than another may seem arbitrary, but I have tried to give a balanced picture overall.

▲ *British Historic Car Racing class events have remained immensely popular. Here Charles Lucas hurls his Maserati 250F sideways round the now defunct Crystal Palace course in London.*

▶ *The Montagu Trophy, presented by the then Lord Montagu of Beaulieu as the team prize for the Gordon Bennett competition in the early 1900s.*

The 'Paris-Bordeaux' Panhard of 1895.

Panhard-et-Levassor

1895, France

The first motor race of all time took place in 1895, from Paris to Bordeaux and back. Panhard promotor Emile Levassor drove throughout that epic 48-hour journey, at the tiller of his Panhard-et-Levassor, powered by a 4 hp, two-cylinder Daimler-Phénix engine. However, during a repeat race in 1896, this time to Marseilles, Levassor lost control in swerving to avoid a stray dog, and was to die the following year reputedly from lingering head injuries.

By 1898 motor racing was under way in earnest – this was the great age of city-to-city racing in western Europe. Building on their moral victory in 1895, Panhard became the most successful marque of the period, and in 1898 their cars dominated the season. Fernand Charron won the Marseilles-Nice and Paris-Amsterdam events; Leys won the Course de Périgueux; and the great *Chevalier* René de Knyff won the Paris-Bordeaux. De Knyff was prime mover behind the Automobile Club de France and he combined his organizational talents with great skill and stamina as a racing-driver.

As you can see, these early racing machines were high-built and spindly, and often with tiller instead of wheel steering. The engine was in the front, coupled to a three-speed gearbox which drove through bevels to a countershaft set across the car with chain sprockets on each end. Chains then drove the rear axle and road wheels. The chassis was wooden, as were the wheels. The early tiller steering had contributed to Levassor's accident. Only the strength of the driver prevented it being deflected by obstacles in the car's path and in 1898 Panhard adopted steering with reduction

gears which lessened this effect. They also adopted a 2.4-litre four-cylinder 8 hp engine that year, plus pneumatic – in place of solid – rubber tyres.

There was no weather protection for the driver and his riding mechanic, who wore heavy protective clothing, often with leather face-masks and mica-lensed goggles for protection against the wind, rain and flying stones. This was a sport for the strong!

Renault Voiture Légère

1902, France

Whereas the Panhard of the 1890s grew larger and larger engines in search of greater power and speed, the Renaults which raced at the start of the twentieth century provided a better pointer to the way racing cars would develop. The first Renault racing cars had appeared in the 1899 Paris-Rambouillet race with shaft-driven back axles and tiny De Dion engines. Louis Renault and his younger brother Marcel were good engineers, and they developed their cars rapidly through 1900–01, increasing engine size and adopting lateral radiators for cooling.

At the time there were effectively four classes of racing car. The French club had formalized regulations in 1901 for cycle-cars below 250 kg in weight; for voiturettes, 250–400 kg; for light cars, 400–650 kg; and for heavy cars, over 650 kg. In effect the light cars and voiturettes became virtually indistinguishable. The Renaults were typical. They ran 499 cc single-cylinder 'thumper' engines in 1900, and for 1902 Renault developed their own power-unit, a 3758 cc four-cylinder.

The 1902 Renaults failed on their début in the Circuit du Nord race, but in their second

Renault Voiture Légère, 1902.

event, the 615-mile Paris-Vienna, Marcel Renault's new four-cylinder machine led the whole field, including the vast heavyweight cars, by reason of its good chassis, better braking and nimble power. In 1903 the great age of city-to-city racing came abruptly to a stop in the Paris-Madrid race, which was abandoned following Government intervention at Bordeaux after a series of crashes which caused at least ten fatalities among competing crewmen and spectators. Louis Renault's light car averaged 90 mph on the straight tree-lined stretch from Bonneval to Chateau-

dun, and recorded 62.3 mph from Paris to Bordeaux. There Louis was informed that his brother Marcel had been killed together with his mechanic after overturning.

Marcel's death brought Renault racing-car development to a brief halt but the company's early-century light cars were shining examples of what could be done with modest engines installed in a light and practical chassis frame.

Mercédès 60 hp
1902, Germany

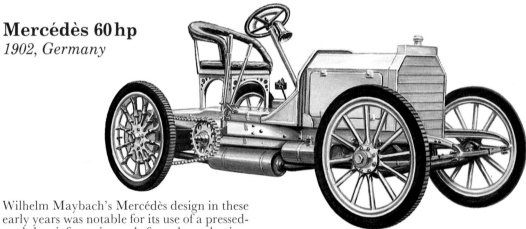

Wilhelm Maybach's Mercédès design in these early years was notable for its use of a pressed-steel chassis frame instead of wooden, selective-gate gearchange of the type still common today, honey-comb rather than gilled-tube radiator, and mechanically actuated rather than atmospheric valve gear.

The cars made their debut in racing trim at Pau in 1901, but failed dismally. The new marque redeemed itself at Nice soon after, where Werner's 5.9-litre 35 hp car covered the flying-start kilometre faster than all other petrol-engined cars, and was beaten only by Léon Serpollet's Land Speed Record Steamer. Werner won the Nice-Salon-Nice race and Mercédès were 1-2-3 at the important La Turbie hillclimb. The 1902 Mercédès com-

petition models used a 6.8-litre engine rated at 40 hp. Although Stead's car won at La Turbie, the 1902 cars did not achieve the great success expected of them and their very advanced mechanical specification, but in 1903 the new 9.2-litre 60 hp model could achieve 75 mph on the very indifferent roads of the time. Mercédès took $3\frac{1}{2}$ minutes off the La Turbie record, and fully 5.9 seconds off the standing-start-mile time along the sea-front record strip at Nice. They were to progress to great things in coming years, including the 1903 Gordon Bennet Trophy race in Ireland which fell to Jenatzy's modified touring '60'.

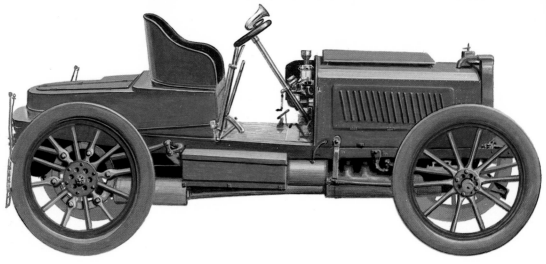

'Gordon Bennett' Napier

1902, Great Britain

Selwyn Francis Edge won the Gordon Bennett Trophy for Great Britain in 1902, driving a green-painted British Napier from the company which he directed and promoted so effectively in these early days.

At the time Britain was virtually nowhere in international motoring and the Gordon Bennett competition was in truth moribund when Edge scored his success. This came in the Paris-Innsbruck section of the Paris-Vienna race in which Marcel Renault performed so nobly, but the nominated French Gordon Bennett team cars all failed on the rough roads and the tough Napier was the sole surviving qualifier to reach the Austrian city.

Edge had promoted Napier through competition since 1900 when he had won a Bronze Medal in the British 1000-Miles Trial with a chain-drive 8 hp twin-cylinder model. He ran a 4.9-litre 16 hp chain-drive Napier in the Paris-Toulouse-Paris race of 1900, and for

1901 Montague Napier developed a monstrous 17,157 cc four-cylinder car for the Gordon Bennett event only to have it debarred for using foreign-made tyres. This car was timed at around 67 mph and won two classes in the straight-line hillclimb at Gaillon. It delivered some 103 bhp but weighed over two tons and proved a barely practical proposition. In fact it was this car which prompted an outright racing-car weight limit of 1000 kg.

For 1902 Napier realized the error of the big-engined way, and turned instead to a shaft-driven light car of only 6.5 litres rated at 30 bhp but delivering closer to 45 in reality.

It was from the chosen dark green livery of the Napiers that 'British Racing Green' evolved as the United Kingdom's recognized international racing colour. While the accepted colour for British cars became green, German cars were white or later silver, French cars blue, Italian cars red, Belgian cars yellow and American cars white-and-blue.

Drivers Jarrott and Stocks with their Gordon Bennett Napiers, 1903.

Mors 'Dauphin'
1903, France

Emile Mors' cars gained immortality with one race victory – and even then it was victory on the only stage actually run of the last city-to-city classic – the 1903 Paris-Madrid which was stopped at Bordeaux. Fernand Gabriel's 70 hp Mors with its boat-prowed wind-splitting bodywork started 168th from Versailles, start order having been decided by ballot. While Louis Renault's light car was the first to reach Bordeaux, it had started third, and was able to run ahead of all others, with an open road stretching far ahead. Renault's time of 5 hrs 29 mins 39.2 secs to Bordeaux represented an average of 62.3 mph. Gabriel had to tear through choking clouds of dust and exhaust fumes, through showers of flying pebbles, past accidents and crash debris, to finish third on the road at Bordeaux, having passed 165 other participants. His time of 5 hrs 14 mins 31.2 secs represented an average speed of 65.3 mph, which subsequently won him the race overall and confirmed this drive as one of the greatest feats in motor-racing history.

The big Mors had weighed in at 995 kg compared to the Renault's 650 kg. Its four-cylinder engine had a bore – the width of one cylinder – of 119 mm and a stroke – the distance travelled by the piston as each combustion forces it down in its cylinder bore – of 165 mm, to give a displacement capacity of 11.6 litres. The engine was carried in a pressed-steel chassis frame with solid axles at front and rear, and transmission was via a four-speed gearbox and chains.

Later in 1903 the Honourable Charles Stewart Rolls (the Rolls of Rolls-Royce) drove a similar 70 hp Mors in a British speed trial at Welbeck and recorded a speed of 84.68 mph (136.28 km/h) over the kilometre. This was a measure of these cars' potential performance. After 1904, however, Mors made little further impact upon the racing scene – Gabriel's heroic performance in that tragic Paris-Madrid being left to etch their name in history.

Gabriel's fantastic Mors, depicted in the Art Nouveau Michelin Tyre building in London's Fulham Road.

Richard-Brasier
1904, France

Georges Richard made Benz-like early cars at Ivry-Port in France before being joined by the ex-Mors engineer Brasier, in 1902. The two men built their Richard-Brasier cars very much after the Panhard fashion of the day; large, heavy and fast. They used steel chassis frames, and while most of their cars employed shaft drive, the very largest – the 40 hp – retained chain drive.

Perhaps Richard-Brasier's main asset was the legendarily consistent and fast driving of Léon Théry. They called him 'The Chronometer' for his even pace on the long-distance race circuits of the day, and more picturesquely *Mort aux Vaches* ('Death to Cows') since he once collided with one such unfortunate animal during a race and was lucky to escape with his life, which was more than could be said for the cow.

After Camille Jenatzy in his Mercedes had won the 1903 Gordon Bennett Trophy for the German team, the German national club organized the 1904 international qualifying event on their home ground, in the Taunus Mountains. There Léon Théry ground round and round to score a notable victory on his big 80 hp Richard-Brasier, averaging 54.5 mph for the 317 miles. His fastest and slowest laps differed by only 90 seconds, over a distance of 87 miles!

The Darracq of 1905 raced with practically no bodywork.

Théry had also won the French Eliminating Trials race intended to decide the year's Gordon Bennett team prior to this race, and in the French club's defence of the Trophy in 1905 his Brasier repeated the double, winning both the Trial and the Gordon Bennett event itself, over an arduous 85-mile circuit laid out around the rugged hills of the Auvergne, near Clermont-Ferrand.

Théry's progress in the Brasier was notably smooth, since Brasier had been one of the first automobile designers to appreciate the importance of controlling spring reactions over bumps, and so to fit shock-absorbers. This combination of smooth and consistent driving and a well-developed and well-controlled motor car certainly paid off for the company in 1904–05.

Darracq
1905, France

Alexandre Darracq had founded the Gladiator bicycle company in France in 1891. He subsequently moved on to build electric cars, briefly, and then in 1898 bought manufacturing rights for the four-wheeled Léon Bollée vehicle. By 1902 his Darracq cars were being produced in considerable numbers, mainly mundane and sombre production vehicles for everyday use, although he was one of the earliest manufacturers to

build really specialized and fearsome vehicles especially for racing, bearing little or no resemblance to his bread-and-butter offerings.

In view of the weight limits on light cars and Darracq's insistence upon running the largest engines he could make, his light cars in 1903 ran bereft of bodywork, their crews sitting wildly exposed on top of a bare chassis frame on wheels, with the radiator and engine open to full view ahead of them. The liberally drilled steel chassis frames carried engines of nearly 5.7 litres, and even the little sister voiturettes ran to 3.8 litres capacity.

For 1904 light-car racing lost significance and Darracq essayed the heavyweight class with 11,259 cc cars for the Gordon Bennett. For 1905 Darracq decided he had gone too far, and opted for 9.9-litre engines in generally lighter and more compact racing chassis,

using modern-style overhead valves in their engine induction systems, and with three-speed gearboxes in unit with the rigid rear axles. As in 1904, the cars were unsuccessful in the gruelling French Eliminating Trials for the Gordon Bennett competition, but Victor Hémery won consolation for Darracq by leading the Circuit des Ardennes in Belgium from Lap 3 to the finish, and in October went on to win the prestigious Vanderbilt Cup race run on Long Island, USA. The big 80 hp Darracq averaged no less than 61.5 mph there for the 283 miles, on very rough roads amidst a vast and unruly crowd.

As a sideline in 1905 the Suresnes company built a 22,518 cc V8-engined sprint car, which recorded 109 mph at Arles-Salon and was later pressed to as much as 117 mph.

Sizaire-Naudin Voiturette
1907, France

Cars bearing this name were designed by Georges and Maurice Sizaire and built by Louis Naudin, pioneers in the development of the small French sporting voiturette. The cars won immediate acclaim for their low price, simplicity and robustness, using a 918 cc single-cylinder engine in a rather dated, armoured-wood chassis frame.

What was startling was their independent front suspension in place of the rigid axle used by most other cars of the time. With a rigid beam supporting wheels on each end, deflection of one wheel over a bump naturally affect the other wheel. With independent suspension, however, the wheels are deflected quite independently of one another, their only

common link being through the steering gear. In the case of the Sizaire-Naudin, the independent front suspension took the form of a sliding pillar on each side, using the outboard ends of a transverse leaf spring as the actual springing medium. While other manufacturers had toyed before with independent suspension, the unusual transmission in which a moveable propeller-shaft engaged in turn with three gear sets of teeth on the crown wheel was peculiar to Sizaire-Naudin alone.

In 1906, the very first full year of manufacture, a Sizaire-Naudin won the important Coupe de l'Auto race for voiturettes driven by Georges Sizaire, a sister car finishing sixth. In 1907 Sizaire-Naudin won the gruelling Sicilian Cup race and repeated the previous year's Coupe de l'Auto triumph, this time coming first and second. In 1908 the company developed the largest of their single-cylinder models, offering a bore of 100 mm and a long stroke of 250 mm to provide a displacement of 1963 cc. They were 1–2 again in the Coupe des Voiturettes and in 1909 came second in the important Catalan Cup race.

The 1907 Sizaire-Naudin with its unusual independent front suspension.

Grand Prix Renault
1906, France

In 1906 the restrictive regulations of the Gordon Bennett competition were swept away in favour of a Grand Prix open to all comers and to be organized annually by the Automobile Club de France. Unlike today when there may be 16 Grand Prix races in a season, in 1906 there was only *the* Grand Prix, run once only, in June. It was not until after World War I that other national Grand Prix races joined the French event on the calendar and became regular fixtures.

Renault won that very first Grand Prix at Le Mans, running not on the famous 24-hour sports-car circuit but on a mighty 64-mile public road course laid out to the east of this industrial city. The winning car was driven by the Hungarian Ferenç or Franz Szisz ('Zizz') who had been Louis Renault's riding mechanic in earlier races and was a works test-driver at the company's Billancourt factory in Paris.

His car was a very conventional 13-litre four-cylinder, and this first victory for Renault in the heavy car class was achieved more by reliability and by steady and competent driving than by sheer speed or animal flair. In addition Renault's long adherence to the shaft-drive back axle did little to aid the car's cornering ability, for the axle itself was not very well located and around corners tended to move in an arc and so create what we now call oversteer—the tail slid wide and tried to spin round ahead of the front wheels. Szisz's driving was sufficient to cope with this shortcoming, and the introduction of detach-able-rim wheels greatly reduced the time lost in slashing punctured tyres away from fixed rims. With detachable rims the whole rim complete with deflated tyre could be un-bolted and replaced by a new rim ready-mounted with an inflated spare cover.

The Grand Prix was run in two parts, six laps each day on both June 26 and June 27 with the cars impounded overnight. Szisz won the first day's racing after 5 hr 45 min 30.4 sec on the road, having averaged 66.8 mph for the 384 miles; on the second day he won again, after a further 6 hr 28 min 36.6 sec on deteriorating road surfaces, to average 63 mph overall for the total 769.9-mile distance. The big Renault won from Felice Nazzaro's Italian Fiat, and Albert Clément's Clément-Bayard. Paul Baras' Brasier made fastest lap overall, on the first day, with an average of 73.3 mph.

Renault did not contest another Grand Prix race until July 1977, when their 1.5-litre turbocharged RSO1 prototype car started in the British Grand Prix at Silverstone.

◀ *One of the ex-GP Renaults during a 24-Hour 'grind' in America circa 1907.*

▲ *Ferenc Szisz's GP Renault defending its victory in the first Grand Prix race of all time, at Dieppe, 1907.*

Grand Prix Benz

1908, Germany

Old Carl Benz considered, once he had perfected his first horseless carriage in 1884–85, that the motor-car as such had been made. He could see very little future improvement upon his invention.

In 1906 this fiercely conservative engineer left the company he had founded to form Benz Söhne with his sons Eugen and Richard. The mainstream concern he left behind immediately developed competition ambitions to publicize its wares.

In 1907 Benz (the original concern) built cars with dual-ignition inlet-over-exhaust engines of 8- and 8.9-litres capacity; this 60hp model became a favourite of Prince Henry of Prussia himself and brought works driver Fritz Erle the important Herkomer Trophy– the Herkomer was in effect one of the earliest sports-car competitions.

Victor Hémery was employed as another factory driver, and he was second in one of these 60s in the Coppa Florio race, ahead of team-mate René Hanriot's sister car. By 1908 Benz were heavily committed to motor racing, and their four-cylinder $12\frac{1}{2}$-litre cars, designed largely by Frenchman Louis de Groulart, served them very well. Hémery won the incredibly rough St Petersburg-to-Moscow race on the model's debut, covering the 438 miles at a staggering average of 51mph. In the Grand Prix at Dieppe, Benz were robbed of victory only by tyre failures and by an eye injury to Hémery who finished second behind Lautenschlager's victorious Mercédès (Mercédès and Benz did not merge until 1926). Hanriot's Benz was third in the Grand Prix with Erle seventh. The cars later went to America where they were raced with enlarged engines, Hémery being timed at over 100mph in the Grand Prix race at

Savannah and finishing narrowly second behind a Fiat. Hanriot was third yet again. In 1909 David Bruce-Brown covered the mile at 109mph in his Benz, now with 15 litres beneath the bonnet.

Lion-Peugeot Voiturette

1908, France

This odd-looking little car was another of the 'Formula 2' voiturettes which abounded in the years before World War I. It was built by Robert Peugeot's company, founded as an offshoot of the main Peugeot family concern still active today.

The single-cylinder 'thumpers' made their major competition debut in the 1906 Coupe de l'Auto, finishing third, and were third again in the same event in 1907.

The way to increase power was in those days believed to be simple enlargement of the engine. The cylinder bore was considered to be quite close to practical and Formula limits, and so the stroke was lengthened enormously, producing the immensely tall engine which characterized the Lion-Peugeots and so many similar cars of this period. To compensate for the height of an engine with a 100mm bore allied to a 170mm stroke, the Lion-Peugeots were low-slung in chassis and body form.

Finally, in 1909, Lion-Peugeot developed the model which became legendary–fitted either with a 100mm × 250mm single-cylinder or an 80mm × 192mm narrow-angle V-twin. The singles had bags of low-speed torque available to punch the cars very rapidly away from slow corners, and they proved admirably suited to most racing circuits of the time. They were driven by Jules Goux to beat the Hispanos into second place in the Catalan Cup, and he won the Sicilian Cup as well. Team driver Guippone beat Goux in Lion-Peugeot's 1–2 success in the Coupe de l'Auto, and so

By 1910 long-strokery reached its height in the twin-cylinder Lion-Peugeot voiturettes, as shown here. The driver and riding mechanic had to look round, rather than over, their car's bonnet.

they went on. Goux also drove the formidable Type VX5 model, fitted with an 80 mm × 280 mm engine, which could achieve 95 mph and whose driver was forced to look around rather than over the phenomenally tall power unit. Michaux also produced a 3440 cc V4 engine of 65 mm × 260 mm and more successes came Lion-Peugeot's way.

By 1911, however, the two breeds of Peugeot were reunited and from that date competition Peugeots had in-line engines, conventional looks and great mechanical sophistication.

'Coupe de *l'Auto*' Hispano-Suiza *1910, Spain*

While the age of monsters lingered on in heavy-car racing, and the world trade recession caused the abandonment of the Grand Prix race from 1909 to 1911, technical innovation was fostered by the Coupe de l'Auto race for voiturettes.

We have already seen how Sizaire-Naudin and Lion-Peugeot fared, but the Spanish-based, French-prepared and Swiss-engineered Hispano-Suiza was perhaps more significant than either in the technical sense. Swiss engineer Marc Birkigt had produced the La Cuadra car in Barcelona in 1900 and was responsible for the Castro car made in that city from 1901 to 1904. The first Hispano-Suiza of 1904 was actually the last Castro renamed. Birkigt would accept second best

in nothing, and his Hispanos became rapidly established as supremely well-engineered and sophisticated cars.

It was in 1909 that the company made its first serious competition effort with a team of 65 mm × 140 mm 1852 cc four-cylinder cars which ran in the Catalan Cup. They proved unsuccessful, but in the following Coupe de *l'Auto* they were placed 5-6-7 and then went on to major hillclimb class victories.

When Lion-Peugeot won the 1910 Catalan Cup, Paul Zuccarelli's now 170 mm-stroke Hispano-Suiza finished third. For the Coupe de *l'Auto* Birkigt lengthened the cars' piston stroke to 200 mm and with 60 smooth horsepower, a great spread of power throughout the engine's rev range and a well-developed chassis, the Hispano-Suiza was victorious. Paul Zuccarelli won, Chassagne was second and Pilliverdier sixth.

In 1911 Marc Birkigt developed a new overhead-camshaft engine which departing engineers Zuccarelli and Ernest Henry subsequently took to Peugeot, and for the 1912 Coupe de *l'Auto* Hispano's Swiss genius planned a team of supercharged cars—ten years before supercharging was to make its mark in motor racing.

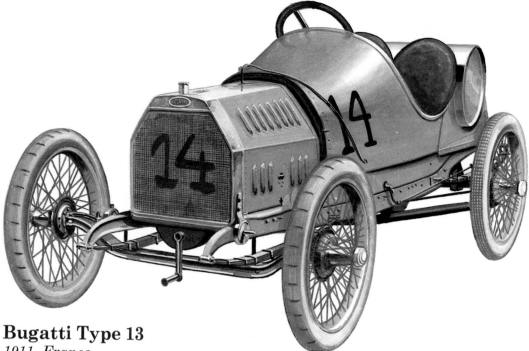

Bugatti Type 13
1911, France

Ettore Bugatti is now a legendary figure in motoring and motor-racing history. The Italian-born French-domiciled artist-engineer produced some of the most aesthetically appealing classic cars of a classic era, and Bugatti as a marque was for many years top of the most-race-wins league.

Bugatti's reputation in competition was founded largely by his Type 13 model, which became known subsequently with its derivative the Type 22 as the 'Brescia', after the Italian venue at which it scored its first major multiple victory.

Bugatti himself had achieved some sporting laurels with cars of his own design but built under other names before he established his own independent factory at Molsheim, Alsace, in 1910. The following year, 1911, saw what became known as the *Grand Prix des Vieux Tacots* ('the Old Crocks' Grand Prix') run on a circuit at Le Mans. Since major manufacturers were not ready for a resumption of formal Grand Prix racing, many dealers and interested sportsmen ran what cars they could find in this event. There, in amongst the mighty chain-drive Fiats, was a team of spidery little Bugatti Type 13s, and Ernest Friderich drove one home into second place overall.

When racing resumed after World War I, modified 16-valve 1½-litre Type 13s reappeared under Bugatti factory colours, Friderich winning the Voiturette Grand Prix at Le Mans in 1920. This brought much publicity to the new marque, and at Brescia in 1921 Friderich

led a Type 13 1–2–3–4 grand-slam victory which won the type its immortal name.

When compared to the other crude voiturettes of the pre-1914 period – the Hispano-Suiza apart – the Bugatti Type 13 was truly a luxury car in miniature, and although it offered only 25 bhp or so, this power was produced in a manner which anticipated the smooth and lively high-efficiency light cars of the thirties. No wonder the Bugatti made such a tremendous impact in 1911, and was good enough to continue very effectively far into the twenties in modernized form.

'Coupe de *l'Auto*' Delage
1911, France

Louis Delage was a flamboyant and wildly extrovert character, and he came to prominence in racing at virtually the instant he commenced motor manufacture – one of his voiturettes with a single-cylinder De Dion engine coming second in the 1906 Coupe de *l'Auto* race.

By 1908 Albert Guyot could be provided with a twin-cylinder De Dion-engined Delage with which to win the Coupe. Delage should have gained much credit for this victory, but since he badly needed De Dion's bonus money he insisted full credit be given them. Work proceeded on producing Delage's own power unit and by 1911 when the factory again contested the Coupe de l'Auto they were using their own three-litre four-cylinder horizontal-valve engines allied to unusual

five-speed gearboxes with an over-drive top ratio.

Paul Bablot, René Thomas, Albert Guyot and Louis Rigal were hired to drive the cars and the first three finished 1–3–4. Bablot averaged no less than 55.3 mph in the winning car, a noble performance which proved to the buying public that the Delage factory could produce cars which were both fast and reliable.

Not that they were very pretty, for the high-set cranked exhaust pipe and ugly bolster fuel-tank on the tail did nothing to improve the car's aesthetic qualities. In deference to regulations demanding bore and stroke di-mensions no more extreme than 78.1 mm × 156.2 mm for the Coupe, Delage had chosen 80 mm × 149 mm and this posed practical problems in filling the cylinder rapidly with gas on each induction stroke. Hence the un-usual valve and exhaust layout. The exhaust emerged from the top of the cylinders due to Delage's chosen use of valves on each side of the cylinder head. The engine gave about 50 bhp at 3000 rpm which was not outstanding, but the cars were very well prepared and driv-en with great skill, and the five-speed gear-boxes allowed the driver to select the most advantageous part of the engine's rev band at each point on the testing circuit.

The magnificent Coupe de l'Auto-*winning Delage of* 1911 *survives to this day in the collection of Sir John Briscoe.*

Grand Prix Fiat
1911, Italy

Of all the early Grand Prix cars perhaps the most sensational-looking in terms of sheer brutishness is the Italian Fiat, built by the Fabbrica Italiana dell'Automobili Torino. In 1907 the Fiat works driver Felice Nazzaro had won the Grand Prix in a 16,286cc 120hp chain-drive model. In 1908 the S61 Grand Prix model was a more modest 10,087cc variant. In 1911 the S74 appeared, with 14,137cc from a four-cylinder 150mm × 200mm engine, chain-driven of course, and fitted with the most sketchy of racing bodies—merely a hutch-like box covering the engine up front, two tiny seats for driver and riding mechanic, and behind that the transverse cylinder of the fuel tank and a rack for four spare tyres.

It was with one of these cars that Louis Wagner fought long and hard against Boillot's new-vogue Peugeot in the 1912 Grand Prix at Dieppe; but in 1911 the S74 had already won the American Grand Prize race for New Yorker David Bruce-Brown at Savannah, Georgia. Bruce-Brown was invited to drive the car again in the Grand Prix at Dieppe and he led the first day's racing, only to be

disqualified on day two for infringing the regulations by refuelling the car away from its allocated service pit.

Bruce-Brown was subsequently killed during practice for the 1912 American Grand Prize race at Milwaukee, Wisconsin, when a tyre burst and threw his big S74 out of control during some high-speed practice laps. Bruce-Brown was only just 22, and had been a national celebrity after winning the Grand Prizes of 1910 in a Benz and 1911 in the Fiat. Now he was a much-mourned national hero.

The mighty chain-drive Fiats continued to be raced in America, notably by 'Terrible Teddy' Tetzlaff, and by Caleb Bragg (normally driving an S61). At least one S74 survives to this day.

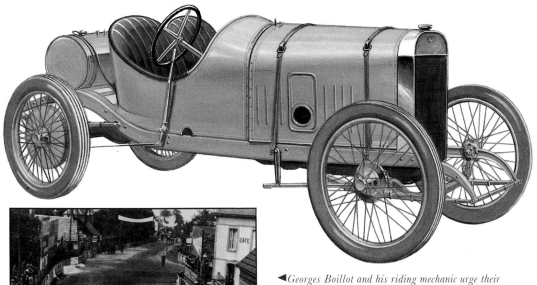

Grand Prix Peugeot
1912, France

Today all self-respecting racing engines feature twin overhead camshafts actuating four valves in the head of each cylinder – two inlets allowing the fuel/air mixture to enter, and two exhausts allowing the burned products to escape. In 1912 Peugeot introduced this basic layout to Grand Prix racing with phenomenal success, their complete dominance lasting into 1913, challenged by Mercédès only at the last gasp in 1914.

Paul Zuccarelli and Ernest Henry had come to Peugeot with Birkigt's Hispano-Suiza ideas, and under the direction of the famous 'Charlatans' team – driver-engineers Zuccarelli, Georges Boillot and Jules Goux – Henry produced the design which was the true progenitor of the modern racing car. The Henry

Peugeots featured shaft-drive instead of chains, and 16-valve four-cylinder engines with twin overhead camshafts driven by bevels. One model for the Coupe de l'Auto had bore and stroke of 78mm and 156mm respectively, to produce three litres, while the corresponding Grand Prix car had 7.6 litres and an output of around 130 bhp at 2200 rpm.

In the Grand Prix at Dieppe the Coupe de l'Auto race was run concurrently, the small-capacity cars mixed in with the Grand Prix cars. The 7.6 Peugeot was a kind of halfway-house between the little voiturettes and the 12–15-litre Grand Prix norm with overweight chassis and normally chain drive. The result of the Grand Prix was a triumph for new over old as Boillot drove his 7.6 brilliantly to beat Louis Wagner's *tacot* Fiat with its 14-litre engine and chain-drive rear end.

The three-litre Peugeot voiturette was retired by René Thomas in this event but Zuccarelli later won the Grand Prix de France at Le Mans with it, and Goux the Coupe de la Sarthe in a 7.6. In 1913 Goux won the money-rich Indianapolis 500-Miles in America with one of these Peugeots, and in 1913 a new 5.6-litre Grand Prix car carried Boillot to his second successive Grand Prix victory. He was the first man to win two Grands Prix, and became a French national hero. For 1914 regulations demanded only 4.5-litre engines, and with four-wheel brakes (unusual at that time) Boillot fought heroically to achieve his hat-trick until the car failed.

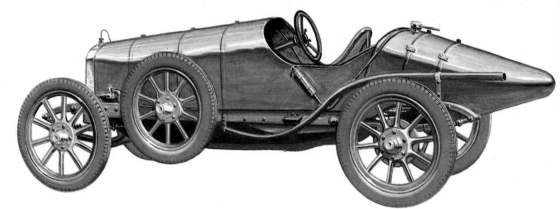

'Coupe de *l'Auto*' Sunbeam
1912, Great Britain

While French marques generally dominated the early years of motor-racing, with occasional intrusion from Germany and Italy, Britain came nowhere in the international league table. But in 1907 the Brooklands Motor Course was opened near Weybridge in Surrey, and with its impetus competition-orientated companies began to make great strides forward, particularly in the design of aerodynamic bodywork demanded by the flat-out high-speed character of the Brooklands track.

Sunbeam began competition in that same year and under the direction of the Breton engineer Louis Coatalen their cars progressed from strength to strength. In 1911 Coatalen produced a Coupe de *l'Auto* car to take on the French and Spaniards at their own game. It was a three-litre car with monobloc (all four cylinders cast into the one piece of metal) engine derived from the production 12/16 hp model. It retired from the prestigious French race, but Coatalen had taken a good hard look at the opposition, and returned in 1912 with a team of four much improved machines.

The 1912 cars still retained side-valves, unlike the overhead valves in vogue with most of the Europeans, but their neat little three-litre engines delivered a reliable 74 bhp. They had Brooklands-derived long-tailed streamlined bodyshells to gain a little aerodynamic advantage over their slab-tailed foreign opposition, and their top speed was up around 90 mph. If only they could survive the race distance, they were bound to be very competitive. In the event, as the Coupe de l'Auto was run concurrently with the Grand Prix they showed very well not only against their three-litre rivals but also against the heavy cars of the Grand Prix itself.

Rigal, Resta and Caillois actually finished 1–2–3 in the Coupe de l'Auto to achieve a British victory which stunned the French establishment, and their cars actually finished 3–4–5 in the Grand Prix! The winner averaged 65.35 mph in the Coupe and this same model later collected over 30 class and outright world speed records, achieving 99.45 mph for the mile. It was the start of great things for Sunbeam – a now devalued name.

One of the fabulously successful 1912 Coupe de l'Auto Sunbeams as it survives today, at the British National Motor Museum, Beaulieu.

Dario Restá hurtling round Dieppe's typically tree-lined country roads in the 1912 Coupe de l'Auto Sunbeam.

The Coupe de l'Auto Sunbeam's four-cylinder, three-litre engine was modest, neat and powerful.

'Indianapolis' Mercer
1913, United States

The Mercer Automobile Company of Trenton, New Jersey, USA, was founded in 1910 and began competition upon the introduction of its rakish Raceabout model in 1911. The marque's early successes were achieved by stripped production chassis but from 1913 a special competition version – the Type 45 – was fielded for contracted works drivers.

In 1912 'Hughie' Hughes had finished third at Indianapolis in the annual 500-Miles Sweepstake event – which was at that time and has continued to be the world's richest individual motor race. His Mercer's engine was smallest in the race, and the car averaged 76.3 mph for the 500-Mile distance. Many other victories came Mercer's way on road circuits like Santa Monica, California, and Elgin, Illinois, and in 1913 the 7292 cc 150 bhp Type 45 racer joined the Type 35-engined 300 cubic-inch class (4916 cc) Model F competition car in the front-line.

Spencer Wishart in a Type F was second at Indianapolis behind Goux's Peugeot, while Ralph de Palma – possibly the most successful racing driver of all time in terms of sheer race victories – won at Elgin, also in a Type F, and achieved three wins from five races entered at San Antonio.

In 1914 Eddie Pullen won the American Grand Prize race at Santa Monica in a Type 45 – the first time that an American car had won this event. Naturally this paid enormous promotional and publicity dividends to the Mercer company, and in celebration the whole Mercer works was actually given a half-day holiday – an unheard-of gesture at that time.

Mercer continued racing until America entered World War I in 1917, and no further competition programmes were attempted upon the return of peace. Still, Mercer are worthy representatives of the budding age of the American competition car, and America's own brand of enclosed artificial track racing was to breed a type of extremely powerful, very fast, and immensely reliable racing machine which in many ways was ahead of European practice during the twenties. Unfortunately the virtual collapse of open-road racing in the USA in that same period meant that the nation could not mount a Grand Prix challenge.

Grand Prix Mercédès
1914, Germany

When the Automobile Club de France issued
its regulations for the Grand Prix of 1914 it
opted for the first time to limit outright engine
capacity, whereas earlier limits had been
applied to overall weight and fuel consump-
tion. The limit was to be 4.5 litres, and the
result was perhaps the greatest Grand Prix
race of all time: 14 manufacturers made
special cars for this one event. Prominent
among them were Peugeot in France and
Mercédès in Germany. Mercédès had won the
1908 Grand Prix upon dogged reliability and
good organization, while in 1912 and 1913
Peugeot, with the immense driving talent
of the flamboyant Georges Boillot, had won
the race on flair and technical innovation and
were now determined to perform the hat-
trick *pour la France* . . .

In Stuttgart, the Mercédès engineers worked on a new 4.5-litre shaft-drive design. The
engines derived from a 1913 six-cylinder unit
with overhead valves and camshaft, hemispherical combustion chambers (this shape
promoted very efficient burning of the fuel/air
charge), dual magneto ignition and four
spark plugs per cylinder to enhance combustion efficiency still further. They adopted a
method of engine construction from contemp-
orary Mercédès aero-engines, building-up the
unit from steel forgings, with the ports welded-
up on bare cylinder heads and sheet water-
jackets then welded carefully round the whole
assembly. This technique replaced the heavyweight casting used previously and eliminated
any chance of failure through the porosity or
weak spots often found in castings.

While these new engines developed around
110 bhp and gave a top speed of some 100 mph
evidence of Mercédès' forethought and atten-

*The four-cylinder engine of the 1914 Grand Prix
Mercedes was copied in essential details by Rolls-Royce
for their World War I aero-engine designs.*

One of the 4½-litre 1914 works Mercédès wheeling round the Lyon-Givors circuit's **Piège de la Mort** *corner during that great Grand Prix.*

tion to detail was also found in the transmission line, where each axle shaft in the rear axle assembly was set at 1° 20′ from the horizontal; this gave an inward camber on the rear wheels and so improved their grip in cornering, the inclination on the shafts demanding individual crown-wheels and pinions to drive each one. What was more, each pinion gear was machined integrally with the halfshaft and each car took with it to France enough half-shafts to give a choice of six final-drive ratios – from 2.2 to 2.7:1. Each was to be tested around the Lyon-Givors circuit, and that which produced the best lap time would be fitted for the race. This spare-no-pains, spare-no-expense attitude to motor-racing success was to become typical of Mercédès when the company returned to racing in earnest in the twenties; the method of engine construction in fact survived into their Grand Prix and sports cars of the mid-fifties.

At Lyon, Max Sailer set the initial pace, tearing round ahead of Boillot's Peugeot before blowing up. Lautenschlager and Wagner then strode implacably forward, to harry Boillot until the Peugeot failed on its final lap. Lautenschlager finished first at an average of 65.38 mph from Wagner and Salzer in sister cars, their German 1–2–3 triumph being received in stony silence by the partisan French crowd. Three weeks later France and Germany were at war – for reasons unconnected with motor-racing and commercial prestige.

The Grand Prix Mercédès were saved during the war; one was studied by Sir Henry Royce in Britain, another was raced extensively by Ralph de Palma in the USA and passed from him into the Packard experimental department. The Rolls-Royce aero-engines which powered the DH4, DH9 and Bristol fighters during that war owed much to the Mercédès.

Christian Lautenschlager's actual winning car survives in England to this day, and is still raced on occasion.

Great Mercs together – on the right the actual winning car from the 1914 Grand Prix and on the left a rebuilt 1937 W125, the most powerful Grand Prix car ever raced. Both survive today owned by British enthusiasts.

Grand Prix Ballot
1921, France

Ernest Ballot was originally a marine engineer and the anchor emblem worn by his cars reflected that fact. Before World War I he had manufactured proprietary engines which he sold to independent chassis-builders, but in 1919 he suddenly appeared with a team of fearsome Peugeot-derived, Ernest Henry-designed Ballot racing cars intended for that year's Indianapolis 500-Miles race.

The Indy Ballots had straight-eight engines, displacing 4.9 litres and using twin overhead camshafts and four valves per cylinder *à la* Peugeot. René Thomas lapped Indy at 104.2 mph in one of these dark blue cars, but Albert Guyot achieved the team's best finish, with fourth place.

In 1920 a new three-litre Formula was adopted in the USA and subsequently in Europe. Ballot built smaller cars to match, which offered around 107 bhp, as against the 125/130 bhp of the 1919 originals. They had front-wheel brakes as standard—most pre-war racing and road cars having relied upon rear-wheel brakes and a transmission brake only, designers considering it dangerous to brake the steerable front wheels. At Indianapolis these smaller Ballots were placed 2–5–7 driven by Thomas, the great De Palma and Jean Chassagne.

In 1921 at Indy again Ballot was out of luck, De Palma retiring after taking $20,000 in lap-leader prize money. At Le Mans for the revived French Grand Prix that year De Palma was in dispute with the autocratic M. Ballot, and held his car back deliberately, finishing second behind the American Duesenberg. Ballot was outraged, claiming moral victory since his cars could run the race distance again as they stood and the American interloper would require a rebuild to cover another yard reliably.

Luck never seemed to be on the side of these handsome cars; the marque had won only one major event, in Italy, when Ernest Ballot himself dropped anchor, and retired.

Grand Prix Duesenberg
1921, United States

Brothers Fred and Augie Duesenberg of Indianapolis began making cars under the Mason name in 1904, Fred having previously been involved with bicycles. Duesenberg Motors was founded in 1913 to produce marine engines, and postwar they concentrated upon competition cars to build an image before embarking on high-performance touring car manufacture.

Fred Duesenberg's first racing car was actually constructed in 1910, using a four-cylinder engine with two horizontal valves per cylinder operated by tall vertical rocker arms which by their movement gained the the name 'walking beam'. By 1912 this engine had been enlarged to produce 100 bhp from 351 cubic inches' (5762 cc) capacity. It pow-

ered Mason racing cars, named after the lawyer who financed the Duesenbergs' operation in Des Moines, Iowa.

In 1914 cars were entered at Indianapolis under the Duesenberg name, drivers Eddie Rickenbacker and Willie Haupt finishing 10th and 12th in the 500-Miles. Later that year 'Rick' won a 300-miler at Sioux City. Before American racing ceased in 1917, the Duesenbergs had gained quite a reputation for themselves within American racing circles, and in 1917–18 the brothers moved their company into a plant in Elizabeth, New Jersey, and built engines for other manufacturers.

In 1919 five 'Dueseys' ran at Indianapolis, and for the 183 cubic inch (three-litre) Formula of 1920, the brothers built new single-overhead-camshaft three-litre engines with three valves per cylinder. Tommy Milton, Jimmy Murphy and Eddie Hearne were placed 3–4–6 at Indy in these cars, and in 1921 Duesenberg's Indianapolis onslaught yielded a 2–4–6–8 result. Then Albert Champion, the French-born spark-plug magnate, financed the team's entry in the Grand Prix at Le Mans, and there Jimmy Murphy made full use of his car's powerful engine, slim-bodied high straight-line speed and excellent four-wheel hydraulic brakes to win despite punctured tyres, holed radiator and literally cooked engine as he crossed the finish line. He drove with his ribs strapped after overturning his car in practice. It was an epic and dramatic drive by any standards, and gave America her first Grand Prix victory–one not to be repeated until 1967.

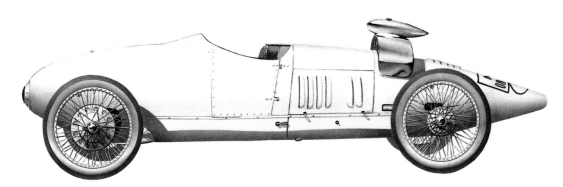

Benz 'Tropfenwagen'
1923, Germany

This extraordinary-looking Grand Prix car was an age ahead of its time, for like the racing cars of today it had its engine mounted amidships between the driver's shoulders and the back axle, and ran independent suspension.

The Mannheim company of Benz decided that 1923 was to mark their final fling in inflation-hit times in an attempt to carry off top Grand Prix honours. Dr Edmund Rumpler designed the car, using a twin-overhead-camshaft, six-cylinder, two-litre engine developing around 80 bhp. He mounted it behind the driver to allow the crew to sit very low in a streamlined body nacelle, and he cooled the engine via a crescent-shaped radiator sitting on top of the car like a saddle. The gearbox offered only three forward speeds, but there were brakes on all four wheels–those at the rear being mounted inboard on the cheeks of the trans-

mission and slowing the wheels via their drive-shafts, as on most Grand Prix cars of the seventies. Rear suspension was laid out on the swing-axle principle, whereby the entire road wheel drive-shaft assembly pivoted about the inboard universal joint on the cheek of the gearbox.

Benz called the car *Tropfenwagen*, or 'Teardrop car', but the team's development programme was delayed and they only made one Grand Prix, the Italian event of 1923 at Monza. Drivers were Willy Walb, Fernando Minoia and Fritz Horner, the latter pair finishing a distant fourth and fifth. At least one of the cars was subsequently fitted with mudguards as a sports car. In 1926 came the merger with Mercédès, and it was not until 1934 that the *Tropfenwagen's* unique layout was mimicked–by Dr Ferdinand Porsche's fearsome Auto Union Grand Prix cars.

Land Speed Record Delage Type DH V12
1923, France

Louis Delage was always seeking potential publicity and promotional exercises; in addition to spending a very considerable fortune on the racing cars which promoted the image of his high-quality tourers, he also invested in some specialized sprint cars for high-speed straight-line work.

Immediately after World War I he authorized construction of a six-cylinder 5136cc sprint and hillclimb car in which René Thomas won the Mont Ventoux climb in 1922 and 1923, breaking the mountain record both times. At La Turbie in 1923–24 he repeated these successes and shattered the record at the Zbreslav-Jiloviste climb in Czechoslovakia to spread Delage fame abroad. A second car was also built with a six-litre twin-overhead-camshaft engine and this was similarly successful, making fastest times at both Mont Ventoux and La Turbie.

Meanwhile, in 1923, Delage produced a massive V12-cylinder car in which two banks of six cylinders each were coupled in 'V' formation upon a common crankcase. This mighty assemblage displaced 10,688cc and produced around 300bhp.

René Thomas drove the car in some major sprint events, such as the hillclimb run every year at the time of the Paris Motor Show at Gaillon, a village between Paris and Rouen.

At Arpajon in 1924 Thomas held the car bravely to record 143.29mph in a sprint meeting, which figure qualified the car as holder of the World Land Speed Record. Within minutes Ernest Eldridge's mighty chain-drive Fiat special *Mephistopheles* (of over 20 litres capacity) went faster but Thomas protested the car since it lacked the regulation reverse gear. This was not very sporting but was typical of French motoring attitudes at that time. Eldridge laboured for two days to provide his special with a reverse gear, and in another run at Arpajon demolished the big Delage's figures.

In 1928–29 Captain Alastair Miller brought the two smaller Delage sprint cars to Brooklands and Thomson and Taylor, the Brooklands tuning and preparation specialists, brought over the big V12. It survives in England today.

Fiat Tipo '805-405 Corsa'
1923, Italy

In 1922 a new capacity limit of two litres was applied to Grand Prix cars. The following year, Fiat emerged with the first successful

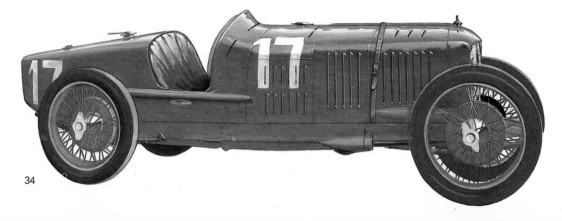

supercharged Grand Prix car. Instead of relying upon atmospheric pressure and the engine's own suction to inspire fuel/air mixture, the Italian car used a compressor pump, or supercharger, to force fuel/air into the engine. The more mixture that could be forced into the cylinders, the more could be burned and therefore the more energy extracted from each individual charge.

Chadwick in America and Hispano-Suiza in Spain had toyed with supercharging before the Great War, and in 1923 Fiat made it fashionable. The straight-eight engines had bore and stroke dimensions of 60 mm and 87.5 mm respectively to give 1979 cc, and with the Wittig vane-type supercharger they developed a quoted 130 bhp at 5500 rpm. With a Roots supercharger 150 bhp was claimed. On their first outing at Strasbourg for the 1923 French Grand Prix the team of 805s all retired, apparently due to road grit and dust drawn into the Wittig superchargers, scoring their internal surfaces and creating loss first of supercharge pressure and then of lubricating oil, and finally internal break-up of the engines.

Fiat put the cars right in time for their national Grand Prix at the new Monza Autodrome just outside Milan, on which artificial circuit the now Roots-supercharged 805s carried Carlo Salamano to victory before an hysterically enthusiastic crowd.

In 1924 Fiat continued to race these cars, Pietro Bordino finishing fourth in the Targa Florio, but all three cars retired from the French Grand Prix and entries were scratched from the Italian. At this time several of Fiat's top engineers had been lured away to join the rival Alfa Romeo company, notably via introductions by a young man named Enzo Ferrari.

The Fiat board was justifiably incensed by the team's being used as a technical training school to foster other companies' racing development. When a 'Fiat-copy' Sunbeam won the French Grand Prix of 1923, and the supercharged '805-copy' Sunbeam won at San Sebastian in 1924 – Alfa Romeo having won the French Grand Prix that year – Fiat withdrew from racing.

Brooklands Lanchester
1923, Great Britain

This was one of the most unusual of the many specials devised between the wars for the high-speed banked Brooklands Outer Circuit. Many of them, such as Count Louis Zborowski's 'Chitty Bang Bangs', and Cobb's Napier-Railton (see page 50) were aero-engine powered. Tommy Hann's Lanchester coupé was rather different. The car upon which he based his striking Brooklands special was a 1911 25 hp Landaulet, running originally as an aerodynamic tandem two-seat saloon and finally as an open single-seater. Hann named the car 'Softly-Catch-Monkey' in its open

form, although the name was not a patch on the original saloon version's imaginative title, 'Hoieh Wayaryeh Gointoo' – apt commentary upon the driver vision afforded by the coupé's arrow-slit windows.

The engine was a 102 mm × 102 mm, 3334 cc four-cylinder unit with horizontal valves, and the car used the Lanchester system of cantilevered suspension, pressure-lubricated epicyclic semi-automatic gearbox and bevel-drive back axle. Tommy Hann found the car 'deafening' to drive, hence the subsequent conversion into an open racer.

Grand Prix Sunbeam
1923, Great Britain

Louis Coatalen of Sunbeam is alleged to have held the pragmatic view that ''Ee ees a wise man who copy wizout altair'. In the twenties, if Coatalen saw an outstanding racing car produced by another company he would unashamedly copy it, paint it green and call it a Sunbeam, or perhaps blue and call it a Talbot, by virtue of the complex Sunbeam-Talbot-Darracq Anglo-French grouping of that period.

Coatalen had long admired the work of Ernest Henry and in 1922 he hired him to produce a new design for Sunbeam. Unfortunately Henry's great creative days–or perhaps more realistically his days as a gifted draughtsman capable of translating others' ideas efficiently into the metal–were over.

With Peugeot, Henry had led the way in 1912. With Ballot he had produced the first European Grand Prix straight-eight in 1919. Now at Sunbeam he chose a twin-overhead-camshaft 16-valve four-cylinder layout, but small piston area and a rev limit of only 4400 rpm rendered the cars ineffective, and they retired from the Grand Prix with valve failures. This Sunbeam model was Henry's last complete design, and with the 1923 Mercédès the last four-cylinder Grand Prix car to appear for a quarter-century.

With his faith in Henry shattered, Coatalen looked to the engineers who had brought Fiat their French Grand Prix victory at Strasbourg in 1922, when the veteran Felice Nazzaro's Tipo 804 had won using a six-cylinder, 65 mm × 100 mm, 1991 cc engine. Coatalen succeeded in attracting engineers Vincenzo Bertarione and Walter Becchia from Fiat, and Bertarione produced the 1923 Grand Prix Sunbeam as a six-cylinder of 67 mm × 94 mm, achieving 102 bhp at 5000 rpm compared to the 1922 Fiat's 112 bhp at 5000 rpm.

At Tours for the French Grand Prix of 1923 the new supercharged Fiats failed and Henry O'Neill de Hane Segrave won for Sunbeam in his 'Fiat in Green Paint'. It was to be the last important GP victory for an Englishman in an English car until the Syracuse Grand Prix of 1955 fell to Tony Brooks and his Connaught.

At the Touraine pits during that historic Tours Grand Prix of 1923; Sunbeam refuels.

Riding mechanic Paul Dutoit has ducked down out of sight as Major Segrave takes the works Sunbeam to victory at Tours, in 1923.

Grand Prix Voisin
1923, France

In many ways the season of 1923 was extra-ordinarily innovative: Fiat adopted super-charging in their Grand Prix cars, Benz produced the incredible *Tropfenwagen*, and in France Gabriel Voisin–the former pioneer aviator and constructor of some 10,000 air-craft during the war years–promoted his motor-manufacturing business by producing the first 'monocoque' Grand Prix car.

Today every Grand Prix car uses a mono-coque chassis, this term being mongrelized from Latin and Greek to mean 'single-shell'. Whereas chassis frames had traditionally consisted of a ladder-like framework of wood or steel upon which engine, gearbox, axles and body were mounted, in a monocoque the bodywork is formed in stressed sheet panelling, and of itself is sufficiently strong and rigid to carry engine, gearbox and suspension loads. A rolled and glued sheet of paper is a monocoque structure. An engineer named Louis Béchereau had devised this type of structure, made from laminated and glued wooden strip, in his Deperdussin racing aero-

plane in 1912.

Eleven years later, Gabriel Voisin applied the idea to his Grand Prix cars for the French event at Tours. His two-litre six-cylinder sleeve-valve engines were underpowered, offering 75 bhp at best, and he sought to compensate by saving weight and wind-resistance. So he formed his cars around a plywood and sheet-metal monocoque chassis structure which doubled as the bodywork in places. In style the cars resembled an about-faced aerofoil in profile, narrow edge forward and deepest point just aft of the two-man cock-pit. The undertray was entirely flat, but unfortunately an ungainly box had to be raised in the front to enclose the engine. Sadly for Voisin his sophisticated cars still proved slow and–worse–unreliable, and the best his team could salvage from the Grand Prix was fifth place.

Not until 1962 would the monocoque structure make an impact upon Grand Prix racing. Voision paid the price of being a prophet before his time.

Grand Prix Sunbeam
1924, Great Britain

His 'Fiats in Green Paint' having won at Tours in 1923, for 1924 Louis Coatalen and his Sunbeam company tackled Grand Prix racing with a supercharged version of their winner.

The engines were still basically Bertarione's 67 mm × 94 mm 'sixes' mounted in modified chassis with the wheelbase extended to 8 ft 6 in and the tracks at front and rear proportionately wider. A disc clutch and four-speed transmission were adopted while in the Wolverhampton test houses, Coatalen and his technical director Captain Irving experimented extensively with a Roots vane-type supercharger blowing compressed air through the Solex carburettor. Eventually they decided that the system was more effective with the supercharger drawing fuel/air mixture from the carburettor, and so Sunbeam became the first European marque to compress mixture rather than air alone. This subsequently became standard practice; in this instance Sunbeam were not mindlessly copying, but actually improving on what had gone before.

The Sunbeam in this form peaked at around 138 bhp at 5500 rpm, and in general characteristics the engine proved slightly stronger than that of the P2 Alfa Romeo at Lyon, where the British cars took the lap record; but the Sunbeams were dogged by magneto trouble and lost the race to the Italians.

Segrave compensated by winning the San Sebastian Grand Prix in Spain later in the year, the last Grand Prix victory of any significance by an all-British car/driver combination until Tony Brooks's Connaught won at Syracuse in 1955; Segrave's Tours victory of 1923 was to be the last major all-British Grand Prix win until 1957.

A team of British green – the Sunbeams at Lyon-Givors, 1924.

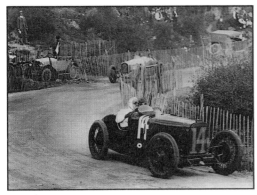

Protagonists at Lyon, 1924, with Segrave's Sunbeam (left) and Campari's Alfa Romeo (right) rounding the tricky Piège de la Mort *corner above the pits.*

Alfa Romeo P2
1925, Italy

The Societa Anonima Lombarda Fabricca Automobili of Milan, Italy, initially made its name in motor racing with cars designed by Ing. Giuseppe Merosi. In 1915 ALFA became part of industrialist Nicola Romeo's empire, and the cars became known then as Alfa Romeos.

One of the company's racing drivers in the early twenties was Enzo Ferrari and this thrusting and aggressive young man was used as an entrepreneur in that period to attract top-line racing car design staff to Alfa from Fiat of Turin. In this, Ferrari was extremely successful, his prize bag being Ing. Vittorio Jano. At Alfa Romeo Jano studied the existing Merosi-designed, production-derived competition cars, and after the failure of an exploratory P1 Grand Prix model he devised the outstanding P2 for 1924.

Jano used Merosi's abandoned 1923 six-cylinder Grand Prix design as a test bed for super-charging experiments, and from it developed the $61\,mm \times 85\,mm$ supercharged two-litre unit for the car which they called the P2, a straight-eight with twin overhead camshafts. The car won the very first Grande Epreuve it contested, at Lyon in 1924 – Giuseppe Campari won the race and an outsize Lyon sausage for his trouble. Campari was a burly, opera-singing driver of outstanding merit, and his team-mate Antonio Ascari was, if anything, an even greater racing driver. That October, Ascari won the Italian Grand Prix at Monza in a P2 producing a claimed 145 bhp at 5500 rpm and in 1925 power output achieved 155 bhp. Ascari won the Belgian Grand Prix at Spa-Francorchamps, but at Montlhéry he ran out of road and was killed while leading the French Grand Prix – the whole team was withdrawn. Brilli-Peri won the Italian Grand Prix that year in another P2 to clinch the World Championship title for Alfa Romeo. Alfa's badge has worn these laurel wreaths ever since.

The six P2s continued to achieve great success in minor events long after the $1\frac{1}{2}$-litre Grand Prix Formula was applied in 1926, bringing Achille Varzi to prominence as a great driver as late as 1930.

Delage 2LCV V12
1925, France

While Fiat were being increasingly frustrated in Grand Prix racing, Alfa Romeo and Sunbeam were poaching talent and innovation, and Voisin and Benz were tackling new methods with little good fortune, Louis Delage's company grew in stature and confidence until the mid-twenties saw it producing some of the most complex, most expensive and most brilliant Grand Prix cars the sport has ever seen.

Delage himself had been grievously disappointed by the failure of his 1914 Grand Prix car, which had been intended to take the marque as triumphantly into this class as others had into the Coupe de l'*Auto* Voiturette competition. The 1914 car had featured four-wheel brakes, four carburettors for the four-cylinder engine, five-speed gearbox and desmodromic – mechanically closed – valves. Now the patron's cousin, Ing. Charles Planchon, designed and built the second Delage Grand Prix contender, nine years after the first.

The two-litre V12 Delage 2LCV was immensely complex, yet built to a frantic time schedule. Drawings were not completed until March 1, 1923, leaving 120 days to build the team cars in their entirety, and to test and develop them. The engine was built and tested in less than eight weeks, the tiny cylinders each measuring 51.4 mm bore × 80 mm stroke and connected to a seven-roller-bearing crankshaft. There were twin overhead camshafts on each bank of six cylinders, and in original form these V12 engines gave about 120 bhp. They resided in orthodox chassis with servo brakes, were very light and compact but too new to do well at Tours.

For 1924 Albert Lory developed the V12, experimentally trying twin superchargers, but at Lyon the team cars ran with atmospheric induction. They were placed 2–3–6 when the Sunbeams and Alfa P2s suffered problems. In 1925 the superchargers were standardized, and with 190 bhp the Delages came 1–2–3 in the Spanish Grand Prix in the absence of Alfa competition and Divo/Benoist shared the winning V12 in the French Grand Prix at Montlhéry, following Alfa's retirement. Louis Wagner was second, and Delage were the toast of France.

◀Louis Delage with his V12-engined Grand Prix car at the Targa Florio of 1926.

▶1926 Bugatti Type 35 in a VSCC club race at Silverstone.

Bugatti Type 35
1926, Italy

Ettore Bugatti believed throughout his life that the cars he sent from Molsheim to race on the circuits of the world should be similar to those he offered for sale to the general public. Fiat, Delage and Alfa Romeo all considered such restraints impracticable and unrealistic. Bugatti was to prove them wrong to a considerable extent.

For the Grand Prix of the Automobile Club de France at Lyon in 1924, he unveiled his Type 35, perhaps the greatest classic beauty of its era. He considered supercharging an Italian trick and an infringement of the two-litre capacity regulations, and since he was Italian by birth few could criticize his comments on jingoistic grounds.

His 1924 Type 35 used a vertical-valve straight-eight engine of 60 mm × 88 mm, 1900 cc, with a built-up eight-section crankshaft revolving in five main bearings. In both construction and effect the Bugatti chassis was a revelation, its side members being tapered fore and aft to offer the greatest section and therefore greatest strength at the points of maximum stress, while the engine contributed materially to its rigidity. Semi-elliptic front leaf springs passed through forged slots in the front axle, which was itself a masterpiece of craftsmanship with its bowed centre section and tapered, upswept extremities. Bugattis had been typified by their quarter-elliptic rear springs reversed forward onto the axle, but in the Type 35 they curved inwards at the tail and were concealed within the beautifully proportioned bodyshell, with its Bugatti horseshoe radiator.

The wheels defied 15 years' acceptance of the spoked-wire type, being of cast alloy with spokes integral with both the rims and the brake drums, thus rendering brake shoes easily replaceable at tyre-change stops. The Type 35 displayed superb handling, magnificent torque and braking, and an essential charm. All these qualities went to make up a revered motor-car.

In 1925 the Type 35 made its real mark winning the first of five successive Targa Florios, and in 1.5-litre form the Italian Voiturette Grand Prix. In 1926 Bugatti supercharged it and won the European Championship, and from 1928 to 1930 the Bugatti 35B in supercharged 2.3-litre form had things more or less its own way in racing everywhere.

The Bugatti cast-alloy wheel, integral with rim and brake drum.

Delage Straight 8
1926, France

After the twelve-cylinder complexities of the 1923–25 two-litre Grand Prix car, Louis Delage authorized Albert Lory to produce a new design for the new 1.5-litre Grand Prix Formula in force during 1926–27. Lory chose to produce another engine of watch-like complexity, with eight cylinders in line and twin overhead camshafts driven from a multi-wheeled gear train at the front of the unit.

While Lory's supercharging of the Planchon-designed V12 cars had employed superchargers mounted on each side of the crankcase, he laid out his 1926 straight-eights with two superchargers slung on the left-side of the crankcase and operated from the cam-drive gears up front. This move placed the exhaust system on the right side of the car with number eight exhaust port discharging very close indeed to the driver's feet.

Since many fatal accidents had involved the riding mechanics mandatory in Grand Prix cars up to 1925, the regulations were changed in 1926, demanding two-seater-width bodies still but allowing the driver to race single-handed. Lory consequently sat the driver of his new car down beside the angled propellor-shaft instead of on top of it, the shaft passing through what would have been the mechanic's lap, and so lowered the new car without infringing the new 31.5in minimum-width rule. This in turn reduced the car's frontal area, reducing the wall of air it had to force before it, and so contributing materially to its aerodynamic efficiency.

Mechanically the 1926 cars proved extremely efficient, the new engines delivering around 160bhp at 6500rpm. In their first season they burned their driver's feet unbearably, but Edmond Bourlier/Robert Seneschal were second at San Sebastian, and Wagner/Seneschal won at Brooklands in the first RAC Grand Prix.

For 1927 Lory revised the cars to place the exhaust on the opposite side to the driver, and they dominated the Grand Prix season, Robert Benoist winning everything in sight. Louis Delage retired his team from racing in 1928 but as late as 1936 Dick Seaman came to prominence in one of these fabulous cars.

The great Dick Seaman winning the JCC 200-Miles at Donington Park in 1936 in his rebuilt nine-year-old Delage straight-eight.

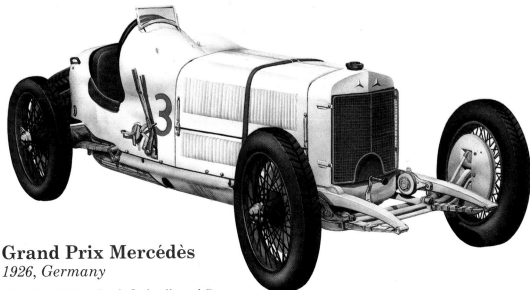

Grand Prix Mercédès
1926, Germany

After World War I only Italy allowed German participation in her motor races. Mercédès took their team of cars there in 1922 for the Targa Florio—including two pre-war 4.5-litre Grand Prix models for Lautenschlager and Salzer, Count Masetti's privately-owned example, two supercharged 28/95s for Sailer and Werner and a pair of new 1.5-litre four-cylinder supercharged cars for Scheef and Minoia. Masetti won the race outright. Mercédès were obviously still very effective.

The company progressed through many minor events until 1924 when Ferdinand Porsche designed for them a straight-eight Grand Prix car of 1980 cc with twin overhead camshafts, four valves per cylinder, sodium-cooled exhaust valves, nine-main-bearing crankshaft and dry-sump lubrication— nearly all features which breathed 'racing' for many many years to come. These engines delivered about 160 bhp at over 7000 rpm but were installed in wickedly handling chassis which won the cars a reputation as driver-killers.

In the cars' debut in the Italian Grand Prix

at Monza, Count Louis Zborowski of 'Chitty-Bang-Bang' fame was killed in one when he lost control and hit a tree. In 1925 Werner used one of the cars to achieve fastest time at the tricky Freiburg Mountain Climb, proving it could be tamed. In 1926 they won the Freiburg, Solitude and Klausen climbs. At the last-named venue a young driver named Rudolf Caracciola ('Karachola') brought his difficult K-type Mercédès to the summit in a time very close to that of works driver Rosenberger in the Grand Prix model. For the inaugural German Grand Prix race on the AVUS circuit at Berlin Caracciola was given a straight-eight and he won with it brilliantly in driving rain.

Yet another bad accident in that race involved a sister car, and in 1927 the Porsche-designed straight-eight was slowly phased out. It gains its place in history for providing Caracciola with the first of his many Grand Prix victories, and for proving Mercédès' postwar engineering skills, despite their mistakes in its chassis design.

Rudi Caracciola and his mechanic acknowledge the plaudits of the crowd after winning the first German Grand Prix, in 1926 at AVUS (Berlin) in the wicked straight-eight two-litre Mercedes.

Fiat Tipo '806 Corsa'
1927, Italy

Having withdrawn from full-time motor racing in pique at having so many of their top engineers stolen by Alfa Romeo and Sunbeam, the Fiat company in Turin set about a return to the sport for promotional purposes in 1926–7. Two notable engineers, Luigi Cavalli and Tranquillo Zerbi, had always remained loyal. When barely 30, Zerbi had been largely responsible for the first supercharged Fiat engine and during 1925 he began work with engineers Sola and Treves on a design for the 1500 cc Grand Prix Formula which was to run through 1926–27. They were attracted by the promise of two-stroke engine power but their advanced test engine exploded repeatedly.

So their back-up design was eventually brought out and dusted-off. This design, which became the startling Fiat 806, was for a twelve-cylinder engine arranged virtually as two straight-six-cylinder units, standing side by side in the front of the car with their individual crankshafts geared together. There were three overhead camshafts to control inclined valves, the common centre camshaft actuating the inlet valves for both six-cylinder units. Bore and stroke were 50 mm and 63 mm, for 1484 cc; it weighed only 381 lbs thanks to extensive use of light-alloy construction, and delivered 187 bhp at 8500 rpm – far more than the 500 lb 170 bhp Delage.

The engine was installed in a wickedly low chassis, with rakish Grand Prix offset-single-seat bodywork and, after initial tests showed the power unit to be fragile, its tune was reduced to give 160 bhp at 8000 rpm.

Cavalli and Zerbi wanted to run the car in the 1927 Italian Grand Prix but Agnelli was not keen to place Fiat's reputation on the 806's unproven shoulders. Bordino was entered in the car in a supporting race at Monza, and won brilliantly, lapping far faster than Benoist's Grand Prix winning Delage. The 806 never raced again, having proved Fiat's point.

Grand Prix Talbot
1927, France

The Suresnes-built Talbots were a product of the confusing Anglo-French Sunbeam-Talbot-Darracq combine during the 'tween-war years, and as profit-conscious shareholders in the British Sunbeam wing of the company would not countenance continued Sunbeam competition programmes in 1926–27, it fell to Talbot to contest the 1.5-litre Formula.

Louis Coatalen was still in charge, with ex-Fiat engineers Bertarione and Becchia responsible for design. In some ways the Talbot Grand Prix cars for the new season were even more advanced than Albert Lory's quite extraordinary Delages. Their straight-eight engines had pairs of forged steel cylinders with welded-on cooling-water jackets and roller-bearing crankshaft, and was offset to the left of the car so that the driver could be placed low down on the undertray, beside the propeller-shaft. The front axle was made in two straight bored-out sections with the springs passing clean through it, the halves being bolted together on the centre-line. What really set the Talbot apart from the Delage was its chassis, which consisted of strong box-members spaced vertically ten inches apart with robust struts welded between them. In addition the whole structure was stiffened by screwing the body panels rigidly to the side members. With over 140 bhp at 7000 rpm, these very light and rigid supercharged cars offered extremely good handling character-istics if their drivers could adjust them properly. Potentially they had the legs of a Delage, despite their power deficit.

Unfortunately front axle failures sidelined the cars in their debut in the 1926 British Grand Prix at Brooklands, but Segrave won the JCC '200' there and the cars were placed 1–2–3 against meagre opposition at Montl-

héry. They did little better in 1927 as the money was running out, and from 1928 to 1930 they raced as Italian private entries. The Talbot Grand Prix car was an outstanding 'might-have-been'.

Maserati 'Sedici Cilindri'
1929, Italy

After the demise of the 1½-litre Grand Prix Formula at the end of 1927 virtual anarchy replaced it during the Depression years up to 1934. It was during this 'Formule Libre' period that a breed of new road-racing specials appeared; those manufacturers who could afford the luxury of motor-racing involvement put the largest possible engines into whatever sketchy chassis frame they could confect.

On July 1, 1929, a new car built by the Maserati brothers in Bologna appeared at Cremona in Italy for a race on the very fast 25-mile public road course there. Baconin Borzacchini–now there's a name to conjure with!–was entrusted with the car and he howled through a 10km timed section of the course to average 152.9 mph–the highest speed ever recorded on a road circuit at that time. The 'Sedici Cilindri' (sixteen-cylinder) Maserati had proved itself the fastest road racing car in the world.

The brothers, Alfieri, Bindo, Ettore and Ernesto, had taken two of their two-litre eight-cylinder engines and mounted them upon a common light-alloy coupled crankcase. Bore and stroke were 62 mm and 82 mm respectively to give 3961 cc. The brothers claimed 305 bhp at 5200 rpm from their monster, which they called the Maserati V4. Alfieri set a lap record of 124.2 mph at Monza and in 1930 Borzacchini won with V4 at Tripoli. It ran poorly without its twin superchargers at Indianapolis and Ernesto shattered the Pescara lap record with them replaced.

In 1931 Ernesto won the Rome Grand Prix with the ageing monster and for 1932 a larger version, V5, was constructed with 4905 cc and over 330 bhp. Luigi Fagioli set a new Monza lap record of 112.2 mph with this car on the revised Milanese circuit and then won the Rome Grand Prix with it. René Dreyfus set a 130.87 mph lap record at AVUS and Fagioli won at Monza. At the end of the year a driver named Ruggeri died in V5 during a record attempt at Montlhéry. During 1933 V5 was slowly rebuilt; with a more modern body style and 350 bhp it reappeared at Tripoli in 1934, driven by Piero Taruffi. He crashed heavily, ending the car's career.

Old V4, rebuilt as a sixteen-cylinder road car, survives today.

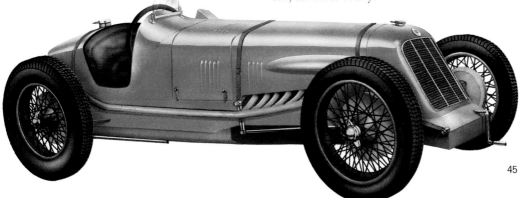

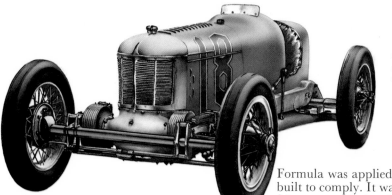

Miller 91
1929, United States

Harry Armenius Miller was a towering figure in American motor racing between the wars.

Miller built carburettors originally, and turned out his first engine in 1916, but it was after World War I that the Miller marque came to prominence. He worked with draughtsman Leo Goossen and works manager Fred Offenhauser to develop the best ideas then current in racing. They drew on Duesenberg's straight-eight engine layout, Peugeot's inclined four-valve-per-cylinder head and twin overhead camshafts, and Ballot's piston-type cam-followers, and produced a three-litre straight-eight of their own which was very advanced and powerful. With this engine in a Duesenberg chassis Jimmy Murphy won the 1922 Indy 500-Miles.

In 1923, 122-cubic inch regulations were adopted to form a two-litre Formula for American racing.

Nine new Millers started at Indianapolis, and four of them finished 1–2–3–4. Miller dominated the rest of the 1923 US track season and although losing Indianapolis to Duesenberg in 1924, won virtually everywhere else.

In 1925 Miller produced his jewel-like front-wheel-drive model which led a Miller 2–4–5–6–7–9 result at Indianapolis. These cars were incredibly fast, Millers taking AAA records at 141.2 mph.

For 1926 a new 91-cubic inch (1491 cc)

Formula was applied and the Miller '91' was built to comply. It was breathtakingly beautiful, a true little single-seater with supercharged engine giving 154 bhp at 7000 rpm, and later, tuned by Frank Lockhart, 285 bhp at 8000 rpm. Lockhart won Indy.

Miller charged $15,000 for front-drive cars, $10,000 for rear-drives; 50 '91s' were built of which perhaps only 12 had front-drive. While the front-drive was faster in a straight line the rear-drive had a better racing record, winning Indy again in 1928 and 1929, while in 1927 Lockhart—later killed attempting the Land Speed Record in a car of his own design—covered a flying mile at 164 mph average. The Millers won almost everything in America in the late twenties, and when showman driver Leon Duray took a pair to Italy for the Grand Prix of 1929 and also ran them at Montlhéry near Paris, Ettore Bugatti took close interest, acquired both cars and adapted the twin-cam head for his own outstanding motor cars.

Alfa Romeo Tipo A 'Bimotore'
1931, Italy

Alfa Romeo were intrigued by Maserati's display of speed and power—though coupled to the usual Bologna unreliability—with the Sedici Cilindri V4, and for 1931 Vittorio Jano drew up a fearsome Formule Libre Grand Prix car of his own, which became known as the Tipo A.

Jano took two of the company's existing and very successful 1750cc supercharged six-cylinder engines and mounted them side-by-side in a style similar to the Maserati V4. The engines were 'handed' so that their exhausts exited respectively on the left and right side of the car, and their crankshafts revolved in opposite directions to counter one another's torque reaction. On the rear of each power unit was a gearbox, with both individual clutches coupled to the same pedal, and there were also two gearlevers, interlinked so that the driver could change with either hand. Two parallel propeller shafts ran to individual bevel-gear final drives for each rear wheel.

The car was completed with the first genuine 'monoposto' (centrally-disposed single-seat) bodyshell seen in a European Grand Prix racing car. The engine dimensions were 65mm × 88mm, giving a total twelve-cylinder capacity of 3504cc and power output of about 220bhp at 5000rpm, although at least 300bhp was claimed at the time.

Grand Prix regulations then asked little more than that race endurance should be not less than a staggering ten hours and on May 24 the new Tipo A made its debut in the Italian Grand Prix at Monza. Unfortunately, Luigi Arcangeli was killed in the car during practice, but the car was repaired and driven by Nuvolari and Borzacchini in the race – where it proved a pig to handle and flopped. Later that year Giuseppe Campari won the import-ant Coppa Acerbo race at Pescara in the car, now better developed and more manageable, and for the Monza Grand Prix two Tipo As were entered for Campari and Nuvolari. Both failed, one with gearbox and the other with tyre troubles and the double-six Alfa was never to be raced again. Even so, they had showed Jano the way ahead.

Bugatti Type 51
1931, France

The stimulus of Maserati did more than merely fire Alfa Romeo into action to replace their obsolescent P2 model, for it crossed the border into France and triggered Ettore Bugatti.

He realized that to maintain his marque's position in the high-performance hierarchy he would have to adopt twin overhead camshafts, and perhaps also subscribe to the cubic-inch theory – 'there's no substitoot for coobic inches' – by building a large-capacity racer in the manner of the Sedici Cilindri Maserati.

'Leon Duray' had sold his two front-drive Miller 91s to Bugatti in part-exchange for three of the Molsheim cars. Thus Bugatti won himself a highly-developed inclined-valve cylinder head with twin overhead camshafts which he adapted first to his 86mm-bore 5.3-litre Type 46 model in 1930, and later with very little alteration to the 60mm-bore 2.3-litre Type 51 for 1931.

In both cases the cylinder head was one with the block, but the 2.3 Type 51 showed 187bhp at 5200rpm compared to the con-ventional 2.3 Type 35T's output of about 135bhp. Bugatti built Type 51s in series, and they completely re-established Molsheim's supremacy during 1931 by winning no less than 11 of the 18 major events held.

Louis Chiron won the Monaco and Czecho-slovakian Grands Prix in 51s; he shared victory at Montlhéry with Achille Varzi; 'Williams' and Conelli won at Spa in Belgium; Varzi won at Tunis; the Polish Count Czaykowski won in Morocco . . . so the list goes on.

The Type 51 looked every inch the true Bugatti it was, with that Type 35-like body design, combining the Grand Prix and high-performance sporting traditions, and cast-alloy wheels integral with the brake drums. In the ten-hour Grand Prix races of the age these contributed materially to success, saving much time during pit stops when brake linings as well as tyres had to be changed. 'Two-three' twin-cam Bugattis raced on all over the world and many Type 51s are still extremely robust and healthy, winning club races to this day.

GP Bugatti with twin overhead camshafts, developed from the Miller 91.

Alfa Romeo
Tipo B

1932, Italy

After the lessons learned with the fearsome Tipo A *monoposto* – literally 'single-seat' – racing car in 1931, Vittorio Jano of the Alfa Romeo factory at Portello, Milan, began development work on a less complex car which would offer little less power but a great saving in weight for 1932. If a new car was to be laid down for Grand Prix racing without thought of turning it into a production model, there was no logical reason to make it anything other than a true single-seater – like the Tipo A special.

Alfa Romeo had generally been racing a two-seat-width 2.3-litre straight-eight supercharged model known as the 'Monza'. Now Jano took this proven engine, added 6mm to the crankthrow to give a bore and stroke of 65mm × 100mm instead of 65mm × 88mm, and so raised capacity to 2.65 litres. New blocks were made with twin superchargers on their left-hand side and Alfa quoted 198 bhp at 5400 rpm from this new unit, which was nothing exceptional. However, the engine gained in terms of torque, its ability to punch the car hard under acceleration, and in a narrow ladder chassis frame and single-seat body of modest weight it was to prove very effective.

Perhaps the most unusual aspect of what in truth was an economy racing car – for Alfa's production at the time was merely ten road cars a week – was Jano's rear suspension arrangement in which the drive was divided along two individual propeller-shafts, one bevel-driving each rear wheel from a central differential mounted on the tail of the gearbox. The reason for this layout has long exercized historians' minds, but probably it was intended to minimize the tendency of the rear axle to hop under acceleration and so cause wheel-spin.

▼ Monopostos *in line astern during the 1935 Dieppe Grand Prix with private owners Dick Shuttleworth, and 'Georges Raph' leading René Dreyfus (temporarily).*

The slim new body was only 26 inches wide with low-cut cockpit sides to give the driver elbow room. The new model—instantly dubbed the P3 by journalists—made its debut in the then five-hour Italian Grand Prix at Monza in June 1932 and it won, driven by Nuvolari. Three more major victories fell to the model that year and then Alfa Romeo bowed to economic strictures at the season's end and left their racing honour in the hands of Enzo Ferrari's private Scuderia, using older models, while the new Tipo Bs were placed under wraps.

When the re-engined Monzas campaigned by Ferrari proved unreliable the Milan management relented and released the *monoposti*. Fagioli drove the first car to victory at Pescara, and he and Louis Chiron rapidly added four more Alfa Romeo victories.

In 1934 the new 750 kg maximum-weight Formula took effect to regularize Grand Prix racing. The German state-backed firms of Mercedes-Benz and Auto Union produced advanced all-independently suspended, supremely powerful racing cars which should have made the solid-axle cart-spring P3s obsolete overnight. An 85 cm minimum-body-width rule led to the *monoposto* cockpit sides being bulged and with 2905 cc engines and 255 bhp they won no less than 13 major events, old 2.6 models winning twice and a streamlined 3.2 litre special once at AVUS.

For 1935 modified suspension, 3165 cc and later 3822 cc power units were adopted to stave off the German horde, but the ageing, by this time immortal cars were generally only successful in the absence of Mercedes-Benz and Auto Union. Nuvolari won the German Grand Prix for Alfa Romeo to grind the German nose into the soil, and the Tipo Bs then became virtually the first recognized historic racing cars. They were the first significant Grand Prix cars to use single-seat, slimline, slipper bodies—the first of a noble breed.

▲*For 1934 and the start of the 750 kg maximum weight regulations a new minimum cockpit width regulation was included. The Alfa* Monoposto's *slim sides had to be bulged to meet it.*

Monoposto *Alfa Romeos prominent on the Monaco Grand Prix grid, Monte Carlo in 1932.*

Gentle giant John Cobb in the cockpit of his Napier-Railton with co-drivers Tim Rose-Richards (left) and Charlie Dodson at Brooklands, 1933.

Napier-Railton Special
1933, Great Britain

John Cobb was a giant of a man, tall and heavily-built, yet extremely modest by nature, very quiet and retiring. He was a wealthy furrier, and his great enthusiasm was for large-engined cars and for racing them on the Brooklands Outer Circuit. For 1933 he contracted Thomson & Taylor of Brooklands to build a very special car for him, using a surplus 23,970cc 505bhp Napier Lion aero engine. This unit was unusual in disposing its twelve-cylinders in three banks of four–what was known as a 'broad-arrow' formation.

Reid Railton designed a massive chassis to accommodate this very powerful yet relatively lightweight engine, using a single-seater body and dispensing with details like front-wheel brakes. One prime target was the world's 24-Hour record, but in 1933 Cobb began his new car's career by setting a 120.59mph standing-start lap record on his beloved Brooklands Outer Circuit.

The first attack on the 24-Hour record failed at Montlhéry in 1934 when Freddie Dixon crashed the car, although in the same year Cobb twice broke the Outer Circuit lap record at Brooklands. In 1935 Cobb, Tim Rose-Richards and Dixon took the 24-Hour record at 137.40mph and at Bonneville Salt Flats in America they also took the Hour record at 152.7mph. The car spent long hours above 165mph and back home Cobb drove it to win the Brooklands 500-Miles at 121.28 mph. In October 1935 he raised the Outer Circuit lap record yet again, to 143.44mph, and that figure was never bettered. In 1936 Cobb and the Napier-Railton raised the 24-Hour record to a stunning 150.6mph and the old car made its swansong appearance in Cobb's hands in 1937, when it won the BRDC 500 once again at Brooklands.

John Cobb went on to take the World Land Speed Record in his twin-engined Railton-Mobil Special. His many friends were grief-stricken when he lost his life on Loch Ness in 1952–his Water Speed Record attempt in the jet-boat *Crusader* ended in the craft's disintegration. The Napier-Railton is still around today, in superb condition.

Auto Union A-Type
1934, Germany

Auto Union was formed by businessman Jorgen Skafte Rasmussen from the German motor companies Audi, Horch, Wanderer and DKW. In an effort to promote their image as high-grade automotive technicians, Auto Union considered building cars for the new 750kg Formula due to take effect for 1934–36. When Ferdinand Porsche approached them with a startling design reminiscent of the ten-year-old Benz *Tropfenwagen*, they said 'yes please' and set about building the cars using

in part a German Government grant authorized by racing-enthusiast Adolf Hitler.

The Auto Union design was unusual in placing the engine between the driver and the car's rear axle, for its V16-cylinder engine layout and for all-independent suspension, which had swing axles *à la* Benz at the rear. The 4.4-litre supercharged but simple (single central camshaft) engine delivered around 295 bhp at 4500 rpm, but with immense torque. The car was clad in a long-tailed teardrop bodyshell.

Early in 1934 Hans Stuck set a class Hour record of 134.9 mph at AVUS and the team was placed third in its first race, again at the Berlin track. Auto Union won the year's German Grand Prix to widespread delight and the Swiss and Czechoslovak Grands Prix too – Stuck humbling Mercedes-Benz in this revolutionary racing car.

For 1935 the Auto Union B-Type appeared, with 4.9-litre 370 bhp V16 engine, Stuck winning the Italian Grand Prix and Varzi the Tunis Grand Prix and the Coppa Acerbo; while ex-motorcyclist Bernd Rosemeyer won the Czech race. The Auto Unions could not match Mercedes this season, their swing-axle rear suspension and immense power making them tricky to handle. However, Rosemeyer was an instinctive driving genius and he tamed the cars better than most. In 1936 he swept all before him, winning the Eifel, German, Swiss and Italian Grands Prix to become European Champion – in effect World

Teutonic fury; the 1937 six-litre supercharged V16-cylinder Auto Union C-Type was fiercely functional.

Champion of the day. His C-Type car had a six-litre V16 engine giving 520 bhp and when the 750 kg Formula was extended through 1937 Rosemeyer won the Eifel, Pescara, Donington and Vanderbilt Cup races; teammates Rudi Hasse and Ernst von Delius took the Belgian Grand Prix and a South African race. From the pen of Dr Porsche had come a fantastic family of sixteen-cylinder cars.

H. P. Muller jumps his C-Type Auto Union at Donington during the legendary 1937 Grand Prix at the Derby circuit in England.

Supercharging arrangements clearly visible in the W25.

Mercedes-Benz W125
1937, Germany

If Auto Union staggered the motor racing world in the thirties by innovation and unconventionality, then Mercedes-Benz refined conventionality to a crushing degree. Mercedes-Benz were also backed financially by the Third Reich, but this Government subsidy went only a little way towards covering the vast expenditure which both German teams made – Mercedes-Benz much more so than Auto Union.

For the start of the new Formula in 1934 design director Dr Nibel laid down the twin-overhead-camshaft W25 straight-eight engine with four valves per cylinder and super-charging, displacing 3.36 litres with bore and stroke dimensions of 78 mm and 88 mm. This unit weighed 450 lb and was supercharged through a system which incorporated a bypass to exhaust blower pressure to the atmosphere when the driver shut the throttle. This caused an ear-splitting shriek which became typical of the cars. While the enlarged Alfa Romeo Tipo Bs had 19.5 bhp per square foot of frontal area and 235 bhp per ton on the start-line, the Auto Union A-Type had 24 bhp per square foot and 260 bhp per ton, and the Mercedes-Benz 30 bhp per square foot and 305 bhp per ton – the German car's modern styling and advanced metallurgy aggravating the effects of Italian financial stringency.

Through that first season the W25's engine size rose to achieve 398 bhp; Fagioli won the Coppa Acerbo and Spanish Grands Prix and shared the Italian Grand Prix victory with Caracciola. For 1935 four-litre engines were standardized and W25s won the Eifel, Tripoli, Monaco, AVUS, French, Swiss, Spanish and Belgian events.

Things went badly wrong in 1936 as Mercedes adopted more powerful 4.7-litre 474 bhp engines in short wheelbase chassis and the result was unmanageable handling reminiscent of the 1924 car at its worst. Caracciola won at Monaco where the tight circuit suited the tail-happy cars, and at Tunis; while that winter saw the driver from Remagen take a new streamlined version with 5.5-litre V12 engine over the mile at 228.05 mph.

For the extra year of 750 kg racing in 1937 the technical office at Stuttgart-Untertürkheim turned out the epochal W125 model, which with a 5.66-litre supercharged straight-eight engine achieved the greatest power output ever seen in Grand Prix racing – 646 bhp at 5800 rpm, a figure yet to be surpassed. In addition a new twin-tube chassis frame was adopted, plus redesigned wishbone front suspension. Two wishbone-shaped components attached the wheel hub assembly to the chassis, controlled by a coil-spring inserted between them. At the rear a De Dion axle layout was adopted. This approach dates from the dawn of motoring in fact, but it is in truth a very practical system: the wheels are connected by a rigid beam serving to keep them parallel at all times in the vertical sense, so resisting the up-edging effect of swing axles whereby a tyre can lean over so much during cornering that its contact patch area with the roadway is drastically reduced.

During 1937 the fearsome W125s proved the ultimate development in 750 kg Formula racing, capable of spinning their rear wheels at 170 mph or more in top gear. Ex-mechanic Hermann Lang won at Tripoli, and in a streamliner at AVUS–lapping at 171.63mph there; Caracciola won the German Grand Prix, Brauchitsch won at Monaco and Caracciola again at Livorno.

The W125s were retained for hillclimb work during the three-litre Grand Prix Formula years of 1938–39 and after the war became prized museum pieces. Outside Mercedes-Benz, one survives today in racing condition, owned by Neil Corner in Britain, and it is utterly beyond price.

Hermann Lang demonstrates the factory's W125 at Montreux in 1978.

Manfred von Brauchitsch in the original 1934 Mercedes W25 Grand Prix car tackling the Kesselberg mountain climb.

ERA
1935, Great Britain

During all these years of development by the Americans, French, Italians and Germans, and since the demise of Sunbeam, Britain had been nowhere on the international racing scene at top level.

Up at Bourne in Lincolnshire, Raymond Mays, son of a local wool-broker, had pursued a long and very successful career of sprints and hill-climbing with occasional races at Brooklands thrown in for good measure. In 1933 he obtained backing from wealthy businessman Humphrey Cook to develop with Peter Berthon a much-modified Riley design they had put together, for use as a true single-seater in international Voiturette or 'Formula 2' racing.

Thus was born the English Racing Automobile, and after conquering minor teething troubles early in 1934 the six-cylinder 1100cc and 1500cc ERAs proved supremely effective. Peter Berthon worked with supercharger expert Murray Jamieson and chassis designer Reid Railton in building the cars.

Only 17 of the basic uprights were built and they raced throughout Europe and in Australia, South Africa and America in the middle and late-thirties. In 1937 ERA was the top-scoring racing make with 14 victories to Mercedes-Benz's seven, although of course the German team achieved theirs in far more august events.

Output of the original 1.5-litre engine was about 150 bhp at 6500 rpm and Mays' personal two-litre model was subsequently developed with Zoller supercharging to achieve as much as 340 bhp. The cars were owned and driven by such famous names as Dick Seaman, Prince Birabongse of Siam–racing under the pseudonym 'B.Bira', Pat Fairfield, Charlie Martin, Peter Whitehead, Peter Walker, Arthur Dobson, Lord Howe and Marcel Lehoux–the last unfortunately losing his life in the only ERA to be totally written off.

Alfa Romeo 12C-36
1936, Italy

In the late thirties once so dominant Italian companies such as Alfa Romeo fought a desperate rearguard action to stem the advance of the better-financed and always more organized German GP teams.

Once it had become apparent that the great Tipo B Monoposto cars were utterly obsolescent, their experimental 3822 cc, 78 mm × 100 mm straight-eight supercharged engines –developing around 330 bhp at 5400 rpm– were installed in modernized all-independently-suspended chassis frames with bulbous, streamlined, slipper bodies similar to those in use by Mercedes-Benz. The result was the 8C-35 Alfa Romeo Grand Prix model, but sadly any improvement the car achieved in handling over the Tipo B still left it barely on a level with the German cars, and of course it lagged way behind them in sheer power.

So a new V12-cylinder engine was developed at Portello and in the shops of the quasi-works Scuderia Ferrari team at Modena. This power unit had dimensions of 70 mm × 88 mm and a displacement of 4064 cc, achieving a claimed output in supercharged form of 370 bhp at 5800 rpm with a considerable increase in torque, smoothness and general flexibility. In practice the improvement was not noticeable.

However, the driving skill of Tazio Nuvolari was always worth several tens of horsepower and in 1936 his 12C beat the Germans in the Penya Rhin Grand Prix at Barcelona, and again at Budapest and in the Milan Grand Prix around Sempione Park. Nuvolari also won the 1936 Vanderbilt Cup in America, using an artificial track laid out around Long Island's Roosevelt Field airport. In 1937 Nuvolari's 12C–36 beat Hasse's Auto Union

in Sempione Park, but fourth place in the German Grand Prix was the best in a major race that year.

Delahaye Type 145 V12
1938, France

If the Italians took a bruising in the late thirties at the hands of the German state-backed teams, then the poor French were utterly pounded into submission. Bugatti steadfastly refused to adopt such trickery as all-independent suspension and virtually faded from the racing scene. Whenever possible the French ran their major races around tightly-chicaned circuits unsuitable for the German cars' speed and power, but when this ruse failed they turned to sports-car racing.

For 1938 new Grand Prix regulations took effect. In place of the 750 kg maximum weight Formula of preceding years, there was now a minimum weight limit of 850 kg for cars limited to three litres capacity supercharged, or $4\frac{1}{2}$ litres unsupercharged. It was apparent that the allowance for unsupercharged engines was inadequate but nevertheless the French Talbot and Delahaye concerns took the plunge.

Hey presto–in the first race of the new Formula at Pau in 1938, René Dreyfus won for the Delahaye truck company, beating the latest Mercedes-Benz on economy. Designer Jean François had produced for Delahaye the Type 45, an ugly V12 of 4482 cc with pushrod-operated valves, De Dion rear axle and four-speed Cotal gearbox. In original trim this truck-like grotesque was to have been a two-seater useable on the road, but in *monoplace* Grand Prix form it achieved around 238 bhp from its unblown $4\frac{1}{2}$ litres and could reach over 160 mph with a long enough run-up. Dreyfus won in the car at Cork, Eire, in 1938, but it was totally outclassed when it faced the Germans again in Switzerland, Germany, and Tripoli and at Donington Park in England. During 1939 the car was utterly outclassed again, although Dreyfus and Varet brought a road-equipped version–fitted with wings and lights–in fourth in the Mille Miglia.

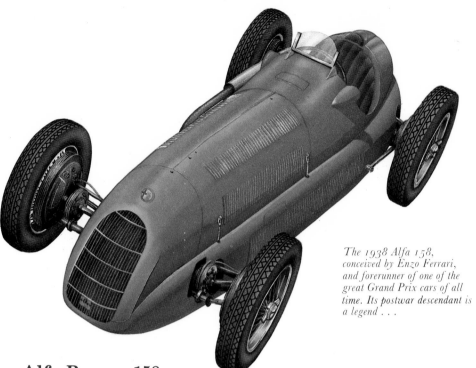

The 1938 Alfa 158, conceived by Enzo Ferrari, and forerunner of one of the great Grand Prix cars of all time. Its postwar descendant is a legend . . .

Alfa Romeo 158
1938, Italy

Enzo Ferrari had been virtually in charge of Alfa Romeo's entire racing operation during the thirties, under the auspices of his private Scuderia Ferrari. This was founded as a commercial self-help concern in 1929 to prepare and maintain Alfa Romeo competition cars–and for a short period other manufacturers' racing motor-cycles–for a circle of wealthy private owners.

Continual failure in Grand Prix racing, however, was doing neither Alfa Romeo nor the Scuderia Ferrari any good. To counter some of Maserati's burgeoning prestige within Italy, Ferrari himself founded a project to produce a 1.5-litre voiturette racing car for the 1938 season.

Gioacchino Columbo–a former assistant of the great Jano–was given the job, and he evolved a 1.5-litre straight-eight engine which was in effect one half of Alfa's three-litre Grand Prix 316 V16-cylinder. However, the gear-train to drive the twin overhead camshafts and other ancillaries on the new engine was placed at its front, unlike the V16 which had the train at its rear and previous Alfa 8s which had it between cylinders numbers four and five.

On the test bed at Modena the new engine gave 180 bhp at 6500 rpm, and by the time of the new car's racing debut at Livorno in 1938 had reached 195 bhp at 7000 rpm. Emilio Villoresi was the driver at Livorno, and he won again in the Milan Grand Prix; but elsewhere the cars failed late that year. Main-bearing lubrication was improved during the winter and in 1939 the 158s offered 225 bhp at 7500 rpm. The Tripoli Grand Prix began the new season, but Mercedes-Benz sprang their secret 1.5-litre V8 W165 model on the shocked Italians and beat them hollow . . . The Alfas retired with overheating in the desert sun, but Farina won at Livorno, Biondetti at Pescara and Farina again in the Prix de Berne. In the Swiss Grand Prix Farina ran second in the rain amongst the German Grand Prix cars!

Racing continued in Italy in 1940, Farina winning at Tripoli, but that winter Emilio Villoresi was killed testing at Monza and promising young Aldrighetti had crashed fatally in a 158 at Pescara. The Alfetta was dominant, but at a price, and in the absence of the Germans.

Mercedes-Benz W154
1938, Germany

With the change in Formula for 1938–39 both Mercedes-Benz and Auto Union developed V12-cylinder three-litre supercharged engines; the Stuttgart engineers produced a unit with twin overhead camshafts per bank, while Zwickau adopted three-cam design with a single, overhead, exhaust-valve cam-

shaft on each bank of six-cylinders and a single, central, inlet-valve camshaft doubling-up for both banks amidships within the engine 'V'.

While Mercedes achieved 420 bhp from their V12, having spared no expense in its design and construction, Auto Union were operating on a very tight budget – even to the extent of using the ex-750 kg Formula cars' gearboxes for their new D-Type three-litre model, and their engine offered about 400 bhp. One major change in the Auto Union was in the chassis design, whereby a De Dion system replaced the swingaxles at the rear.

Through 1938 the Mercedes-Benz cars were dominant, following their initial surprise defeat at Pau, in France. Auto Union missed races while completing their development, and were reeling from the loss of Rosemeyer in a record-attempt that winter; Mercedes' W 154 models were therefore placed 1–2–3 at Tripoli, Dick Seaman won the German Grand Prix, Lang won in Italy and so on.

Auto Union finally appeared with their neat new cars and Nuvolari to take Rosemeyer's place; the Italian master won the Italian and Donington Grands Prix for the team. But in 1939 Mercedes adopted two-stage supercharging, in which a small compressor fed a larger compressor and then the total boost was applied to the engine; the V12 developed 480 bhp in this form and Lang was dominant with the W 154/163 rebodied model. Seaman died in his car in the Belgian Grand Prix while leading in the rain. Auto Union adopted two-stage supercharging in time for the 1939 French Grand Prix at Rheims, H. P. Muller winning for them, and Nuvolari drove to win the last pre-war Grand Prix of all, at Belgrade on the day war was declared between Germany and Great Britain. Mercedes-Benz, who by the end of 1939 had been approaching 1937 lap speeds, revived their 1939 cars to race in Argentina in 1952.

Donington Grand Prix 1938 with Muller's Auto Union D-Type V12 holding off Von Brauchitsch's Mercedes-Benz W154 V12 – mid-engine design versus front-engine.

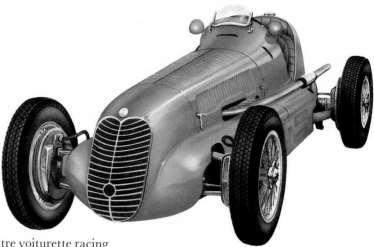

Maserati 4CL
1939, Italy

Maserati found that 1.5-litre voiturette racing was a much more sensible proposition for a factory such as theirs during the thirties. In the face of ERA opposition from Britain they eventually achieved a dominance in that class and a degree of Italian national prestige which led Alfa Romeo once again to react to the Maserati brothers' stimulus and turn to building a new voiturette themselves. Since the Italians could not play in the same park as the big boys – the German teams – they took their ball away . . .

Maserati introduced their six-cylinder 6C model for voiturette racing in 1936, replacing the formal four- and eight-cylinder models. In general design it followed on from the eight-cylinders but the twin-overhead-camshaft 1493cc power unit was good for 155 bhp at a smooth 6200 rpm. From 1936 to 1938 the Maserati 6C was very competitive with the similarly six-cylinder ERA and in Italian national events and most others around Europe it numerically saturated the field.

It was in response to the success and prestige achieved by these 6Cs that Alfa Romeo weighed in with their straight-eight Tipo 158 voiturette in 1938; to combat its threat the ever-cheerful and willing Maserati brothers produced in turn their 4C, using the 6C chassis to carry 1088 and 1496cc twin-overhead-camshaft engines. Still the Alfetta proved to be streets ahead, and in 1939 the 4CL was released with four valves per cylinder.

As the 'Sixteen-valve' Maserati this model became famous, as did its 'square' dimensions of 78mm × 78mm to give 1489cc, and its supercharged power output of 220 bhp. However, while the Maserati won everywhere not attended by the Alfetta team, it could not combat the 158s on equal terms. But postwar, Maserati would be back, with modified versions of this late-thirties voiturette . . .

'Boyle Special' Maserati 8CTF
1939, Italy

Maserati actually led the German Grand Prix of 1939 for a time, the three-litre supercharged straight-eight driven by Paul Pietsch sorting out the German cars on the opening lap. But fiercely accelerated and braked as is necessary on a road circuit, it never had the stamina to maintain the lead. The high-speed constant grind of the Indianapolis 500-Miles track race, with left-turns only over a $2\frac{1}{2}$-mile rectangular course containing four banked 90-degree corners, was a different type of challenge; here the 8CTF was to shine.

The brothers had built the 8CTF using virtually two 4CL sixteen-valve four-cylinder 1.5-litre engines coupled in tandem to form a 2990cc unit giving about 355 bhp. One car was bought by Americans and ran at Indianapolis in 1939 as the Boyle Special, being driven by the local ace Wilbur Shaw. The car set new performance standards at the Speedway, with its independent front suspension and well-located live rear axle, and Shaw won handsomely. In 1940 he returned with the same car and won again, with similar ease. Since the USA was still not embroiled in World War II, there was another Indy 500 race in May 1941, and Shaw was all set to achieve a staggering hat-trick of victories driving Boyle's famous car. Before the race Shaw had some misgivings, and sure enough he lost the lead when a wire wheel broke its spokes and collapsed; the leading Maserati spun heavily into a retaining wall and damaged Shaw's spine.

After the war this remarkable old car was revived and raced again at Indy by Ted Horn. He placed it third in both 1946 and 1947, by

which time the Miller-based Offenhauser engines used as standard by the American track community were being installed in 'roadster' cars, based palpably upon the Maserati which had brought such revolution in 1939.

Maserati 4CLT/48
1948, Italy

In 1938 the surviving Maserati brothers, Ernesto, Bindo and Ettore (Alfieri having died after a bodged appendicitis operation) sold control of their company to industrialist Count Omer Orsi. The factory was moved from Bologna to Modena (although Maserati's badge always retained the trident symbol of the city of Bologna), and with a sound financial base produced many of its four-cylinder voiturette models.

In 1946 revived 4Cs were in the forefront of motor racing's reawakening, and the design was quickly developed with two-stage supercharging and with a tubular chassis frame in place of the former girder type. These developed models were known first as the 4CL, then with the tubular chassis as the 4CLT. At all times the independent front suspension had been by wishbones and torsion bars, with quarter-elliptic leaf springs carrying a rigid axle at the rear. In 1948 the 4CLT appeared in its definitive form with coil-springs for the front suspension tucked inboard out of the airstream and operated by extension lever arms attached to the wheel-hub carriers. This 4CLT/48 model was raced by the quasi-works Scuderia Ambrosiana team and sold well to private entrants.

In their debut two 4CLT/48s were placed 1–2 at San Remo, driven by Alberto Ascari and Luigi Villoresi. The model was known as the San Remo Maserati ever after. Villoresi won four more major races that season, and was second to Wimille's Alfa Romeo in the Italian Grand Prix, beating a new V12 Ferrari in the process. In the winter of 1948–49 4CLT/48s raced in the Argentine Temporada series, a virtual unknown named Juan Manuel Fangio scoring an early international success in one. When Alfa Romeo withdrew for the 1949 season, Maserati briefly assumed their mantle before being overtaken by Ferrari's V12s. Fangio made his name in Europe with a 4CLT, while drivers like Reg Parnell, 'B. Bira' and Dr Farina all won for the trident.

By 1950, however, the claimed 260 bhp of the 78mm × 78mm, 1490cc engine was achieved at the expense of oil-oozing unreliability. The old engine had reached the end of its development and although still competitive in club racing events the Maserati 'fours' were now non-entities at Grand Prix level.

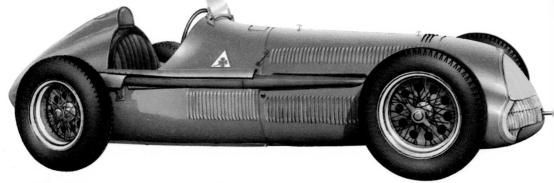

Alfa Romeo 158/159 Alfetta
1947–51, Italy

German industry was shattered by World War II. Auto Union was apparently finished for ever as a motor-racing force and Mercedes-Benz, although its plants were in the Western zone of influence, was in no state to race a bicycle, never mind the most complex Grand Prix cars the world had ever seen. Italy, however, had not suffered such severe destruction, and there is something in the happy-go-lucky Italian character which makes sporting achievement and general enjoyment of life far more vital than any political aim or commercial success.

Consequently the Italian firms of Alfa Romeo and Maserati were well-placed to resume racing the moment peace settled in Europe. In fact Alfa Romeo had continued competition testing and development into 1942 and when the German Army took control in northern Italy in 1943 the seven extant Alfetta 158s were holed-up beyond reach in a remote mountain cheese factory.

In June 1946 two 158s were entered for the St Cloud Grand Prix in Paris. Farina and Jean-Pierre Wimille both led, both retired and established a total team failure unique for Alfa Romeo in this post-war period. The following month saw four 158s at Geneva, two with two-stage supercharging which were placed first in Farina's hands and seventh for Varzi. At Turin Varzi and Wimille were placed 1–2; at Milan Count Trossi, Varzi and mechanic Sanesi were placed 1–2–3.

In 1947 a Grand Prix Formula was recognized allowing $1\frac{1}{2}$ litres unsupercharged. This admitted prewar cars, all that was available, and made a fairer match than the pre-war comparative capacity limitations. Alfa Romeo's 158s entered four events and won all four, normally producing 275 bhp at 7500 rpm while an enlarged low-pressure-supercharger engine gave over 300 bhp for the first time.

Come 1948 and Alfa's season started with the Swiss Grand Prix at Berne, where in practice Varzi was killed in only his second-ever racing accident; but Trossi won the race, and Wimille followed up with victory in the French, Italian and Monza Autodrome Grands Prix to become recognized

◀ *Juan Manuel Fangio of Argentina, five times World Champion Driver, in his works Alfa Romeo 159 Alfetta at Silverstone, 1951.*

as the outstanding driver of his day. Tragically that winter saw Wimille crash fatally in Argentina at the wheel of a Simca-Gordini and Trossi die of cancer. Alfa's driving team had been gutted, and the company withdrew from racing for 1949, in part due to development time required by postwar production projects, and the need of funds to pay for this work.

In 1950 Alfa Romeo returned in force with their famous 'Three Fs' team of Luigi Fagioli, Giuseppe Farina and the new Argentinian ace, Juan Manuel Fangio. Fangio won at San Remo, Monaco, Spa, Reims, Geneva, and Pescara while Farina was victorious at Silverstone in the British Grand Prix (opening round of the newly-instituted World Drivers' Championship competition), Berne, Bari, Silverstone (for the International Trophy race), and in the Italian Grand Prix at Monza. He narrowly beat his team-mate to clinch the World Drivers' Championship title.

During that year, however, Ferrari's unsupercharged V12 cars, initially in 3.3-litre form and progressively growing towards a full $4\frac{1}{2}$ litres, had pressed Alfa Romeo hard, and for 1951 the 159 model appeared with a staggering 42.6 lb supercharger boost and 425 bhp at 9300 rpm on the test-bench. In this form the cars did about 1.6 miles per gallon and were therefore bloated with extra fuel tankage. Still they had to make one and sometimes two refuelling stops during a Grand Prix distance race, while the slightly

▲ *Works Alfa Romeo team in the woodyard at Berne's Bremgarten circuit, prior to the 1948 Swiss Grand Prix.*

▼ *The fearsome frontal aspect of the Alfetta was a grim warning for drivers of lesser cars when it loomed in their mirrors.*

slower, unsupercharged cars were capable of running through non-stop, or with one quick top-up at most.

The cars took 11 first places during the new season, but at Silverstone Gonzalez beat them at last and shattered Alfa's utter supremacy with his unsupercharged Ferrari 375 V12. Fangio became World Champion, however, and Alfa Romeo retired from the Grand Prix scene they had graced for so long. They returned eventually in 1979.

Talbot-Lago Type 26C
1948, France

The old and honoured name of Talbot was sustained by Italian-born Major Antoine 'Tony' Lago who joined the dying Sunbeam-Talbot-Darracq combine in 1933. He managed the famous Talbot-Darracq works at Suresnes and when the combine collapsed in 1935 he found backing to establish an independent Automobiles Talbot company. Looking at the firm's '23CV' six-cylinder production engine, Lago considered it had competition potential and engineer Walter Becchia applied to it an overhead-valve cylinder head with hemispherical combustion-chambers. The resulting 160 bhp four-litre engine brought Talbot back into sports-car racing in 1936. In 1937 the team won four of seven races including the second French Grand Prix for sports cars. In 1938 the French race reverted to true Grand-Prix-car status, and a single stripped sports Talbot was the only other finisher behind the Mercedes-Benz flotilla – 48 miles behind. . .

For 1939 Suresnes built offset-single-seater 4½-litre Grand Prix cars plus a brand-new central seat *monoplace* intended for a new three-litre supercharged V16 engine designed by Becchia. Lago never found finance to build this unit so the normal six-cylinder was used instead. Raymond Mays retired the single-seater from the 1939 French Grand Prix when its fuel tank split. Just three days after peace with Japan ended World War II, Raymond Sommer drove the Talbot-Lago *monoplace* to second place in a race at the Bois de Boulogne.

In 1946 Louis Chiron drove the ageing car to some fine places and won the revived French Grand Prix with it in 1947. Louis Rosier gave a new Talbot-Lago its debut in the 1948 Monaco Grand Prix, the engine now featuring two high camshafts and producing some 240 bhp at 4700 rpm. A Wilson pre-selector gearbox was used (as in the ERAs) and in 1949 the 9 mpg economy of the powder-blue cars told against the 3–4 mpg of the supercharged 1½-litre Italian machines. Rosier won the Belgian Grand Prix, Chiron the French, and Etancelin, Guy Mairesse and Sommer three

other big events. In 1950 Rosier won the Dutch Grand Prix and at Albi, and with wings and lights, won the Le Mans 24-Hours for sports cars. Fangio won the Rafaela 500 in one of these cars and in 1951 Rosier won the Dutch Grand Prix again. Lago's 'trucks' are still racing today.

Ferrari 125
1949, Italy

In 1938 Alfa Romeo withdrew Scuderia Ferrari's sanction to run their racing operations from their remote base at Modena, and brought their racing activities back home to Portello, Milan. The yellow shield and black prancing Horse badge of Ferrari was removed from the cars, and replaced by the green *quadrifoglio* (four-leaf clover) on a white triangle to identify the new works Alfa team.

Enzo Ferrari was taken on to direct operations, but he disliked close control from the Alfa Romeo management and disputes reached a head in his resignation. Part of his severance agreement was that he should not enter racing with any car other than an Alfa Romeo, and when his new Auto Avio Costruzione company did build a couple of 1.5-litre straight-eight sports cars for the 1948 Mille Miglia they were entered simply as '815s' with no marque designation whatsoever. One was driven by Alberto Ascari, son of the late Antonio Ascari of Alfa Romeo P2 fame, and when Ferrari began building cars under his own name in 1946–47 Ascari was again enlisted to drive them.

Ferrari used Alfetta draughtsman Gioacchino Colombo to design his first cars, choosing the power potential and low internal stress offered by a V12 engine layout. Unfortunately the first Tipo 125 V12 was not as powerful as had been hoped, so it was installed in a tiny, abbreviated little chassis which proved to handle diabolically badly. Then, when Alfa Romeo withdrew for the season of 1949 and the Ferrari 125 chassis was lengthened

to tame its handling, Ferrari soared to fame.

The ubiquitous Farina had scored Ferrari's first Formula 1 victory with a 125 at Lago di Garda in 1948 and during 1949 Alberto Ascari developed his driving under the tutelage of team-mate Luigi Villoresi (brother of the late Emilio of Alfa 158 fame); Ascari won the Swiss and Italian Grands Prix while 'Gigi' (as Villoresi was known) won the Dutch event. In 1950 Ferrari turned his attention to unsupercharged engines, designed by his new chief engineer Ing. Aurelio Lampredi.

BRM V16
1950, Great Britain

Just before World War II ERA Ltd had been torn apart by a gentlemanly difference of opinion between Raymond Mays and his technical partner Peter Berthon on the one hand, and the financial backer Humphrey Cook. Mays and Berthon had gone off to launch a scheme to put Britain into Grand Prix racing with a car backed by the best firms in the motoring business.

War delayed the project, but in 1945 Mays gained industrial backing, notably from Alfred Owen and Oliver Lucas. Thus British Racing Motors was formed, to develop an ambitious V16 1.5-litre GP car with Rolls-Royce centrifugal supercharger.

After innumerable delays and problems in austere post-war Britain, the first car was unveiled in December 1949. The V16 engine had a shallow 135-degree vee angle, displaced 1496cc and could produce a stunning 450bhp at 10,000rpm or more. But BRM's project floundered through bad management, overconfidence and under-finance; when it made its over-publicized debut at Silverstone in 1950 and broke on the grid, bitterly misled British enthusiasts jeered and tossed coins into its cockpit. Reg Parnell drove one car to a club race victory at Goodwood that season and in 1951 two cars were placed fifth and seventh in the British Grand Prix, driven by Parnell and Peter Walker. But BRM could not sustain entries in Grand Prix races and when Alfa Romeo withdrew at the end of that season there were no reliable 1.5-litre cars remaining. For 1952–53 Grands Prix were run for two-litre unsupercharged Formula 2 cars, and the V16 became reliable too late.

Cooper-Norton '500' F3
1950, Great Britain

Immediately after World War II a tremendously dynamic movement began in Britain to promote a formula for 'poor man's motor racing'. It all revolved round the idea of building sketchy little four-wheel chassis carrying 500 cc motorcycle engines amidships, behind the driver, so that a direct chain drive to the rear axle could be retained, exactly as on the parent motor-cycle. The most popular engine available was the single-cylinder or 'one-lunger' Norton 500, and from its earliest origins in the Bristol area this form of racing spread vigorously; it crossed the Channel into Continental Europe, reached the USA, and eventually became recognized internationally as Formula 3.

Colin Strang and Clive Lones in Britain were two father-figures of this type of racing and in 1946 Charles and John Cooper, father and son, began copying their pioneering efforts by building 500s from chopped Fiat 500 chassis frames powered by Speedway JAP engines. After minor teething troubles the prototype 550 lb Cooper-JAPs proved most successful. In 1948 a batch of Cooper Mark 2s were offered for sale, with early customers and race winners including Stirling Moss, Peter Collins and Stuart Lewis-Evans. One-litre Cooper hybrids were offered with 988 cc HRD or 996 cc JAP engines while the Norton became standard in Formula 3 trim; in the years 1951–54 Formula 3 Coopers won 64 out of 78 major international races for the class. The Mark 6 model of 1952 used a tubular chassis frame in place of the original box-section affair

and in 1955 the Mark 9 adopted disc brakes.

Essentially the mid-engined, transverse leaf-spring all-independent suspension theme was continued unchanged through these years, and in establishing their dominance the Cooper Car Company of Surbiton, Surrey, virtually killed competition within the Formula. When a 1.5-litre Formula 2 class was promulgated for 1957, Charles and John Cooper 'inflated' their mid-engined layout, with its excellent weight distribution and nimble handling, to accommodate a four-cylinder Coventry Climax car engine, and the writing was on the wall for the classical front-engined racing car.

Ferrari 500
1952, Italy

While the number '500' in a Formula 3 Cooper's title indicates that it had an engine of only 500 cc, the figures in this Ferrari's title form part of the Modenese company's unusual car classification system, used for many years. Ferrari classified their cars by the number of cubic centimetres of one engine cylinder. Thus the Ferrari 500 of 1952–53 was a two-litre four-cylinder Formula 2 car, with each cylinder displacing 500 cc: 500 cc × 4 = 2000 cc. Similarly the earlier 1.5-litre supercharged V12 Tipo 125 car had had a unit cylinder displacement of 125 cc: 125 cc × 12 = 1500 cc.

Aurelio Lampredi had developed the simple four-cylinder twin-overhead-camshaft two-litre engine for Formula 2 racing in 1950 and it was installed in a conventional twin-tube chassis frame with transverse leaf-spring, independent front suspension and a De Dion axle layout at the rear. When 1.5-litre supercharged Grand Prix competition died at the end of 1951, organizers were allowed freedom

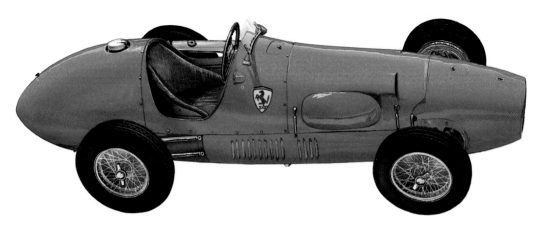

by the International governing body – the Commission Sportive Internationale – to throw their World Championship Grand Prix races open to unblown two-litre Formula 2 cars. Ferrari, wily as ever, had a well-proven design ready to go.

With the 90 mm × 78 mm, 1980 cc, 170 bhp Ferrari 500, Alberto Ascari proved virtually unbeatable in these two seasons, taking two successive Drivers' World Championship titles. In 1952 he won every Grand Prix he started, six of them, and in 1953 he won five times in eight starts. The only major Grand Prix he did not contest in 1952 fell to team-mate Piero

Taruffi in a sister Ferrari 500; and in 1953 newcomer Mike Hawthorn won the French Grand Prix and Dr Farina the German event for the Prancing Horse team. It took Fangio to break Ferrari's stranglehold by winning the last two-litre Grand Prix, at Monza at the end of the 1953 season.

Add to this magnificent success story non-Championship race wins at Syracuse, Marseilles, Saint-Gaudens, La Baule, Pau and Bordeaux, and you can appreciate how the news of another 'Ascari, Ferrari' victory became repetitious in those two remarkable years.

Maserati A6GCM
1953, Italy

When two-litre unsupercharged Formula 2 cars became acceptable for Grands Prix when the Formula was changed for 1952–3, Maserati's spearhead was a development of the sports-racing A6G six-cylinder engine first produced in 1947. Gioacchino Colombo reworked it, and for 1952 it gave 165 bhp from 1988 cc. Maserati often ran Ferrari close – the

more so in 1953, with handsome new bodies and the driving of Argentinians Juan-Manuel Fangio and José Froilan Gonzalez. Success came finally at Monza, where Fangio won Maserati their first Italian GP victory.

This was an emotional moment, and it was from the A6GCM car – often erroneously referred to as the 'A6SSG' – that the archetypal front-engined Grand Prix car of the nineteen-fifties, the Maserati 250F 2.5-litre six-cylinder, was subsequently developed for competition in 1954–60. The initials 'GCM' indicated 'Ghisa' – iron (cylinder block – which by this time was light alloy!); 'Corsa' – racing; 'Monoposto' – single-seater.

The Cooper-Bristol took the great Mike Hawthorn to his first major successes.

Cooper-Bristol T23 Mk 2
1953, Great Britain

While Cooper Cars built mainly mid-engined Formula 3, Formule Libre and sports cars well into the mid-fifties, the advent of unsupercharged two-litre Formula 2 racing gave Charles and John Cooper the idea of moving up the motor-racing ladder. The BMW 328-derived Bristol six-cylinder engine was adequately powerful for most competition purposes, was readily available and also very reliable at this time, so the Coopers father and son decided to build a car round it for international Formula 2 racing.

Since the six-cylinder engine was quite long it was considered impractical to install it in the mid-car position behind the driver, and so a conventional layout was adopted, with the engine up-front. The 66mm × 96mm, 1971cc, pushrod overhead-valve engine delivered about 127bhp and 5800rpm, and in Cooper's tough box-section chassis frame with independent suspension front and rear by wishbones and transverse leaf-springs, it performed adequately.

Three cars made the type's debut at Goodwood on Easter Monday, 1952, the hitherto virtually unknown Mike Hawthorn bursting to stardom by winning two races in one of the cars, while Alan Brown won a third.

Through the rest of the season Hawthorn went from strength to strength in his Cooper-Bristol and won himself a Ferrari works drive in 1953. He was the first Englishman to drive for a top Continental works team since Dick Seaman, who drove for Mercedes-Benz in 1937–39.

For 1953 a Mark 2 Cooper-Bristol was built around a tubular chassis frame and again proved very popular with British private entrants including Ken Wharton, Alan Brown, and Ecurie Ecosse–the Scottish team for whom Jimmy Stewart drove regularly. Jimmy had a kid brother at home more interested in clay-pigeon shooting than in motor racing; his name was Jackie . . .

Kurtis KK500A
1953, United States

Colorado-born Frank Kurtis began building competition cars in the early thirties, and his company, Kurtis Kraft, was firmly established in 1938, building technically innovative single-seaters for US midget-class and National Championship track racing in large numbers, including Indy '500' winners of 1950–51 and 1953–55. He built the Cummins Diesel 1952 Indy qualifying car, and the legendarily successful centrifugally supercharged Novi V8s. From 1949 some ugly sports cars also emerged. Over 2000 Kurtis Kraft chassis were built, the last front-engined roadster in the early sixties.

In 1953 and 1954 Bill Vukovich won the Indy '500' in the 'Fuel Injection Special' owned by Howard Keck, qualifying at average speeds of 138.392 and 138.488mph respectively! Jack McGrath, in another KK500 chassis, qualified at 141.033mph in 1954 to take pole position. Poised for the hat-trick, 'Vukie' was killed in the 1955 '500', involved in another driver's accident.

Mercedes-Benz W196
1954, Germany

Mercedes-Benz returned to racing after World War II as early as 1952; in that year they took three of their 1939 W154/163 three-litre V12 Grand Prix cars to Argentina but were humbled by Froilan Gonzalez handling a modern two-litre Ferrari on a very tight circuit. At Le Mans, Frenchman Pierre Bouillon, driving a Talbot as 'Levegh', tried to cover the 24-Hours single-handed and when in his fatigue he made a mistake with 30 minutes to go, Hermann Lang and Fritz Reiss won the race for Mercedes in a 300SL coupe.

A new 2.5-litre unsupercharged Grand Prix Formula was to begin in 1954 and, spurred on by their Le Mans success, Mercedes-Benz – as usual – spared no expense in preparing for it. They developed their W196 model to employ a brand-new straight-eight engine with desmo-dromic (mechanically closed) valve gear and Bosch fuel injection; the whole unit was slanted over steeply to one side in order to allow minimal bonnet height. The engine was mounted in a multi-tubular spaceframe chassis with torsion-bar suspension, and was mated to a five-speed gearbox in unit with the rear axle. The M196 engine (Mercedes-Benz used 'W' for 'Wagen' to indicate the car overall, and 'M' for 'Motor' to indicate the engine alone) had dimensions of 76mm × 68.8mm, giving 2.49 litres, and it developed around 270bhp. The German engineers also adopted all-enveloping fully streamlined bodywork with the driver seated centrally in a spacious cockpit.

The cars were late in appearing, finally making their debut at Reims for the French Grand Prix in mid-summer 1954. They won,

of course, with Fangio at the wheel of the winning car and Karl Kling's sister W196 second. In three hours or so Mercedes-Benz had again set new performance standards in Grand Prix racing.

At Silverstone the poorly marked turns troubled the drivers of the streamlined cars; for the German Grand Prix a conventional slipper body was adopted and Fangio won. Fangio also won the Swiss and Italian Grands Prix and, with his early-season successes for Maserati being taken into account, was World Champion. During 1955 Mercedes-Benz went from strength to strength, using Moss alongside Fangio, plus Kling, Hans Herrmann and Piero Taruffi as drivers. In the British Grand Prix at Aintree Moss led a Mercedes W196 1–2–3–4 finish, and at the end of the year the team withdrew – having proved their superior skills once more.

◀ *The slipper-bodied exposed-wheel W196 swept all before it through the greater part of the 1954 and 1955 Championship seasons.*

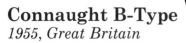

Connaught B-Type
1955, Great Britain

The non-Championship Syracuse Grand Prix, held in Sicily late in 1955, formed an historic landmark in motor racing. The amateur driver Tony Brooks–a dentist by profession–took on the might of the works Maserati team in his under-financed British Connaught and beat them on their native soil. It was the first time that a premier-Formula Continental Grand Prix of any kind had been won by a British driver at the wheel of a British car since Segrave's success for Sunbeam at San Sebastian in 1924.

Rodney Clarke and Kenneth McAlpine–of the famous building family–had founded Connaught Engineering in 1947 to build a sports car for McAlpine to race. They used a 1767 cc Lea-Francis engine and the car went so well that customers queued up for replicas.

Engineer Mike Oliver was one customer, and in 1950 he assisted in building a prototype Formula 2 car using the 'Leaf' engine in modified form. For 1951 nine Formula 2 Connaught A-Types were constructed; the engine was now developed virtually beyond recognition from its Lea-Francis parentage, displacing 1964 cc from 79 mm × 100 mm, and producing 140 bhp at 6000 rpm. The Connaught chassis were excellent, with good balance and handling, but they never had the power to achieve dramatic results.

Then for the new 2.5-litre Grand Prix Formula of 1954 Connaught adopted the Alta four-cylinder engine and clad it initially in a strikingly advanced all-enveloping stream-lined body, enclosing the wheels and with a central, single seat. This body was quickly discarded for practical rather than technical reasons and replaced by a normal slipper body, and it was the Connaught in this form that took Brooks to his historic success at Syracuse.

The B-Type 2.5-litre Connaught was known as the 'Syracuse' model thereafter, but industrial sponsorship in sufficient sums never came the company's way and despite some really very enterprising engineering and futuristic schemes which later proved quite realistic and workable, Connaught floundered from one financial crisis to the next and finally collapsed in 1957.

Lancia D50 V8
1955, Italy

Ex-Alfa Romeo engineer Vittorio Jano designed for Lancia a long line of very advanced production cars which handled supremely well; then, for the new 2.5-litre Formula of 1954, the company authorized him to produce a team of full-blown Grand Prix cars. His design was as original as the Mercedes-Benz W196 but had little in common with it.

Jano laid out a V8-cylinder 2.5-litre engine of 76 mm × 68.5 mm and alternatively 73.6 mm × 73.1 mm, finally opting for the longer-stroke unit. Each block of four cylinders had twin overhead camshafts, and four double-choke carburettors provided one inlet to each cylinder. Jano mounted this unit in torsion within his lightweight multi-tubular space-frame chassis in order to add stiffness to the structure; to obtain minimum handling change during a race as full fuel tanks became empty, and to concentrate the car's essential mass well within its wheelbase, he outrigged the tankage in sponsons on each side.

With as much as 295 bhp at 8500 rpm claimed for this Lancia V8 engine and a very small and light overall package, much was expected from the D50 model; and with the driving team of Alberto Ascari, Luigi Villoresi and Eugenio Castellotti it proved immensely fast. The car handled tremendously well; but once it had been pushed beyond its limit the evenly balanced front and rear ends tended to lose adhesion all at once, and almost before the driver knew he was close to the borderline he would find himself spinning wildly into a ditch. Ascari shone at Barcelona on the car's debut at the end of 1954 and won at Turin and Pau in 1955, but

at Monaco he crashed luridly into the harbour after losing control at the quayside chicane, having inherited the race lead at that moment. He was pulled out of the water unhurt, but within the week crashed fatally while trying his hand in a sports Ferrari at Monza.

This grievous loss was compounded by financial problems at Lancia, and late in 1955 Gianni Lancia ceded the whole of his racing department to the beleaguered Ferrari concern. Ferrari ran much-developed versions of the D50 with more predictable handling through 1956 and 1957, before replacing it with the Jano-designed V6 Dino in 1958. In 1956 Fangio and Lancia-Ferrari won the World Championship titles.

Maserati 250F/1
1957, Italy

Gioacchino Colombo and Alberto Massimino were responsible for the immortal 2.5-litre six-cylinder Maserati Grand Prix car which proved so widely popular in the 1950s Formula. Maserati at Modena went into virtual mass-production of these cars, over 30 being constructed, all eventually sold into private hands. Characteristically, Maserati had always supplied privateers with cars, often before their own works team vehicles were completed, and this was so with the 250F.

Introduced in 1954, the model won its first race, the Argentine Grand Prix, driven of course by the great Juan Manuel Fangio. Later that year and throughout 1955 the cars were generally outclassed by Mercedes-Benz in Grand Prix racing, but they were generally next best, and they utterly excelled in the many minor non-Championship Formula 1 events run in Europe at that time.

The 250F used a multi-tubular spaceframe chassis of the current vogue with double-wishbone and coil-spring front suspension and a De Dion rear end with transverse leaf-spring. A neat gearbox was in unit with the final-drive assembly between the rear wheels and the 84 mm × 75 mm 2.49-litre six-cylinder engine with twin overhead camshafts and three twin-choke carburettors produced around 260 bhp.

In 1956 Moss drove for Maserati, having campaigned a private 250F to such effect in 1954 that he had won his Mercedes-Benz drive for '55. Moss won at Monaco in 1956 but Fangio was too good in the Lancia-Ferrari and won the Championship. Then in 1957 Fangio rejoined Maserati–his second love after Alfa Romeo–and in a classical season won the Argentine, Monaco, French and a tremendously dramatic German Grand Prix to clinch his fifth and final World Drivers' Championship.

During that year a 68.5 mm × 56 mm 2449 cc V12 engine was tried in 250F chassis but follies in sports car racing cost Maserati dear and they were forced to pull in their horns for 1958. Some lightweight 'Piccolo' Maserati 250Fs were built, in one of which Fangio ran his last race–the French Grand Prix of 1958– and 250Fs in private hands raced on even into the very last 2.5-litre Grand Prix, the US event in 1960.

Vanwall VW1-VW10
1957, Great Britain

From the British viewpoint, the 1957 British Grand Prix was the most significant event of postwar motor racing, for Stirling Moss and Tony Brooks gave Vanwall its first Grande Epreuve victory, and Britain her first-ever home win. Thus started over 20 years of British domination in Grand Prix racing.

Tony Vandervell, industrialist head of the Vandervell Products bearings concern, was the man behind Vanwall. He had been involved with the BRM V16 project in its early days but characteristically became impatient with the dilly-dallying and time-wasting he saw there.

Consequently he bought a series of Ferrari unsupercharged V12 Grand Prix cars which his men progressively modified and fiddled with to form the series of 'ThinWall Special' Ferraris in which drivers like Mike Hawthorn, Nino Farina and Peter Collins charged to several Formule Libre race victories.

For 2.5-litre racing in 1954, Vandervell hired Cooper to build him a simple front-engined chassis, into which was fitted an entirely new two-litre four-cylinder twin-overhead-camshaft engine developed very largely from Norton racing-motorcycle experience – Vandervell being a director of that company. He called the car the 'Vanwall Special'. In 1955 the ephemeral 'Special' tag was dropped; the car became 'Vanwall' pure and simple, and by this time had a full 2.5-litre power unit.

It was obvious that the Cooper chassis was not up to much, and for 1956 Vandervell hired the best people to modify the design. He used Colin Chapman of the burgeoning Lotus Company to design a very light and efficient,

true-spaceframe multi-tubular chassis, and Chapman's colleague, aerodynamicist Frank Costin, produced the unusual teardrop body seen here. Moss drove the new Vanwall to win a minor Formula 1 race at Silverstone first time out but was not available for the rest of the season since he was contracted to Maserati. Harry Schell shone at Reims, the Vanwall running among the Ferrari fleet for lap after lap and giving them a very nasty fright indeed.

Vandervell was not afraid of going abroad for good components, and his very powerful four-cylinder 96 mm × 86 mm, 2490 cc cars used German Bosch fuel-injection, Goodyear US-patent disc brakes and so on.

For 1957 Vandervell signed on Stirling Moss, the almost equally talented though less easily motivated Tony Brooks and the very promising but frail Stuart Lewis-Evans to drive his 280 bhp cars, and they came into their own with victory at Liverpool's Aintree circuit. Moss went on to win the Pescara Grand Prix and then the Italian Grand Prix. This gave Vandervell immense personal satisfaction – it had always been his avowed ambition 'to beat those bloody red cars' . . .

In 1958 Vanwall were far and away the top team and won six of the ten Championship-qualifying races – Moss winning the Dutch, Portuguese and Moroccan Grands Prix and Brooks the Belgian, German and Italian. Lewis-Evans was every bit as fast as his illustrious team-mates but lacked the stamina for very long races, and tragically sustained fatal burns when his engine blew up at Casablanca in the final race of the year.

There the Championship had to be decided between Moss and Hawthorn, Vanwall and Ferrari, and while the Drivers' title went to Hawthorn, Vanwall achieved the World

Constructors' Championship.

Vandervell had proved his cars, his British cars, the best in the racing world; but with his health failing, and deeply affected by Lewis- Evans' death, he withdrew from competition thereafter – only one or two half-hearted entries following from Vanwall until they dried up completely in 1961.

▲ *Tony Brooks at Silverstone in a 1958 Vanwall showing off its glorious lines and scientifically designed air intake and exit systems.*

◄*Frank Costin's glorious high-tailed teardrop body on the Vanwall played a major part in the car's 1957–58 success story.*

Cooper-Climax T51
1959, Great Britain

In 1955 Cooper built some little central-seat mid-engined sports-racing cars, using a single overhead camshaft four-cylinder Coventry Climax fire-pump engine of 1100cc. They were very successful, the engine was ideal for racing purposes and the Coventry company was keen to help. In 1956 development began for a new 1.5-litre Formula 2 due to take effect in the following year, and a dress-rehearsal race at Silverstone saw a new single-seater Cooper-Climax victorious using a 1460 cc Climax engine driving through a modified Citroën gearbox. Roy Salvadori was the driver, and in the Oulton Park Gold Cup later that year he repeated the success.

In 1957 Cooper put this Formula 2 T43 design into production, using a new twin-overhead-camshaft four-cylinder Climax engine known as the Type FPF, and displacing 1475cc. Cooper-Climax cars won eight of the ten Formula 2 events that year and private entrant Rob Walker had a special 1960cc engine made which powered Jack Brabham's Cooper into sixth place at Monaco in the marque's Grand Prix debut. Salvadori drove

a similar car home fifth in the British Grand Prix. Then came 1958 and the rear-engined revolution really got under way . . .

Stirling Moss's Walker-entered 1960cc Cooper-Climax won the Argentine Grand Prix. With a further enlarged 2014cc Climax engine Maurice Trintignant won the Monaco Grand Prix in a Walker Cooper–two in a row for the baby cars. Then the factory cars of Brabham and Salvadori adopted 2.2-litre engines with further promise, and Leonard Lee of Coventry Climax authorized production of a full 94mm × 89.9mm 2495cc engine delivering some 239bhp at 6750rpm. This was standard in Cooper T51 and Lotus Formula 1 cars in 1959 and Jack Brabham won the World Championship in a Cooper-Climax. In 1960 his new lowline Cooper-Climax T53 proved even more effective, and the Australian won five Grands Prix in a row to clinch his and Cooper Cars' second consecutive World titles.

By that time the mid-engined theme was well-established, front-engined racing cars were looked upon as dinosaurs from a bygone age, and a fundamental change in the face of motor racing worldwide had come about.

Cooper Cars graduated from 500cc motor-cycle-engined F3 to 1500cc Formula 2 and eventually 2½-litre Formula 1 racing with mid-engined tiny and nimble cars like this.

Stanguellini FJ
1959, Italy

While 1.5-litre Formula 2 racing formed a very logical rung on the motor-racing ladder just below Grand Prix racing with its 2.5-litre cars, the gradual demise of 500cc Formula 3 racing had left no 'starter's Formula' in the international scheme of things. In an attempt both to provide a practical form of poor-man's motor racing and to form a bottom rung for the ladder, the Italians adopted in 1958 what they called Formula Junior, for cars using 1100cc engines closely based on standard production road car parts. The Stanguellini was a product of this Formula.

Formula Junior was introduced internationally in 1959 and ran until 1963. Naturally since they had created it, the Italians were initially dominant with pretty, scaled-down 'Maserati 250Fs' and the like, using Fiat or Lancia engines mounted in the front of conventional little road-racing *monoposti*. A typical Stanguellini-Fiat of the 1959 era would have offered 70bhp from its 1089cc four-cylinder Fiat engine. Then in 1960 Lotus developed their boxlike Type 18 Formula Junior, Formula 2 and Formula 1 family of cars, Cooper was also using a mid-engine layout, and so Formula Junior was as brutally revolutionized as had been Formula 1 before it. The British teams utterly destroyed the international market for cars from small Italian firms such as Stanguellini, Wainer, Branca and Taraschi; and Lotus, Cooper, Elva, Lola and the like scooped all the orders. When Jack Brabham left Cooper to build his own cars in 1962 his Brabham-Ford FJs quickly gained remarkable popularity and the Ford 1100cc engines developed notably by Keith Duckworth and Mike Costin of the Cosworth Engineering concern quickly came to rule the roost.

By the time the Formula ended in 1963 the Ford 'screamers' were producing closer to 120bhp and the difference in chassis and suspension sophistication between the front-engined 1959 Stanguellini and the mid-engined 1963 Brabham was like night and day. Britain's increasing motor-racing strength lay in her chassis designers, and so it remains to this day.

Not the prettiest racing car ever but effective in its day – the Italian Stanguellini-Fiat ruled the roost in Formula Junior in its formative years of 1958–59.

Porsche Type 804
1962, Germany

After many years' participation in sports car events, Porsche found their way into Formula 2 racing during the seasons of 1957–58, using central-seat versions of their 1.5-litre flat-four-cylinder RSK sports-racers. For 1959 the Stuttgart-Unterturkheim company produced 'proper' Formula 2 cars with single-seat slipper bodies and torsion-bar suspension; having raced successfully throughout 1960 they were well-prepared for the new Formula 1 introduced in 1961 – effectively the familiar 1.5-litre 1957–60 Formula 2 regulations, with extra weight and safety restrictions.

During 1960 Dan Gurney and Jo Bonnier drove these Porsche Type 718 cars regularly and they proved quite competitive, their air-cooled 85 mm × 66 mm engines delivering about 155 bhp at 7500 rpm. But they had neither the power nor the handling actually to win anything, and for 1962 a flat-eight-cylinder air-cooled Type 804 model replaced these bulky 'Old Ladies' of the Grand Prix world.

The Type 804's beautifully made engine, with a massive cooling fan perched above it, had bore and stroke dimensions of 66 mm and 54.5 mm respectively to provide 1498 cc, and it delivered a claimed 185 bhp at 9200 rpm. Dan Gurney shone in the new silver cars even though, in truth, the Porsche had the power and handling characteristics of a road-going VW Beetle. With a little luck he won the 1962 French Grand Prix at Rouen for the German team; he dominated the German Grand Prix at Nürburgring in terms of sheer pace but when it rained could not improve on third place. On Porsche's door-step in the non-Championship Solitude Grand Prix just outside Stuttgart, Dan and Jo Bonnier sent 350,000 German spectators wild with delight by finishing first and second in the teeth of strong British opposition.

But Porsche found it hard to justify the budgetary outlay involved in making racing cars unlike those they produced for sale, and at the end of the 1962 season they withdrew. Despite immensely expensive sports-car racing projects in succeeding years, Porsche have, at the time of writing, yet to return to the white heat of Grand Prix competition.

Jo Bonnier in the works flat-eight air-cooled Porsche 804 during the 1962 British Grand Prix at Aintree.

BRM P57 V8
1962, Germany

After the disasters of the V16 BRM, the original BRM Trust sold out the company complete to Alfred Owen's private industrial combine, the Owen Organization, who developed the V16 to competitive form for minor Formule Libre events and during the later fifties ran a new 2.5-litre four-cylinder P25 Grand Prix design in World Championship events. Yet again enthusiasm exceeded practicality and success was limited until 1959 when Jo Bonnier won the Dutch Grand Prix in one of the cars. By the end of 1961 BRM did not have another victory in anything significant, and Sir Alfred Owen's brother Ernest and the other members of the family board were making noises about the small fortune being absorbed by BRM's continued operation.

Sir Alfred made it clear to BRM's personnel that 1962 was a make-or-break season. They were to win something substantial, or the team operation would be folded up. Peter Berthon had designed a 1.5-litre V8 engine known as the P56 for the new Formula, and this was subsequently developed by ex-Rolls-Royce engineer Tony Rudd and mounted in a spaceframe chassis and body of his design,

known as the P57. It appeared in practice for the 1961 Italian Grand Prix and impressed as one of the smallest and prettiest Formula 1 cars ever seen.

Early in 1962 the car won the first heat of its debut race, the Brussels Grand Prix, driven by Graham Hill. It went on in Hill's hands to win at Goodwood and then again in an epic near-dead-heat with Jim Clark's new Climax V8-powered Lotus 24 at Silverstone. The World Championship season opened at Zandvoort for the Dutch Grand Prix and Graham won in magnificent style. Hill fought a season-long duel with Clark and Lotus for the Championship titles; he and BRM triumphed, with victories in the German, Italian and South African Grands Prix. In 1963 Hill won at Monaco and in the United States Grand Prix, and team-mate Richie Ginther excelled once more.

The V8 spaceframe BRMs continued to provide private entrant service into 1965 with their 68.5 mm × 50.8 mm, 1497.7 cc engines giving 188–202 bhp at 11000 rpm. These engines also powered other chassis by Lotus, Brabham, BRP and Scirocco-Powell.

Graham Hill at Goodwood in 1962 demonstrating why the new V8 BRM was nicknamed the 'Stackpipe' at that time.

Lotus-Climax 33
1964, Great Britain

Colin Chapman put his Lotus Engineering company in the forefront of advanced motor racing during the fifties with a series of very lightweight and aerodynamically efficient sports-racing cars. He was expert in building multi-tubular spaceframe chassis of which every single frame component was put to work in either tension or compression. It was this expertise that won him the Vanwall consultancy contract during 1955, and in 1956 he introduced his own prototype single-seater Lotus, a front-engined device aimed at Formula 2 and using a Coventry Climax FPF four-cylinder engine.

In 1960 he took to the mid-engined configuration with the Lotus Type 18, and its performance set the standards of the day, shaking even Cooper's grasp on Formula 1 in non-Championship events, if not in World Championship rounds. Stirling Moss won the Monaco Grand Prix that season in Rob Walker's private Lotus-Climax 18, and won the Monaco and German Grands Prix in a similar Walker car in 1961. At the end of that year Innes Ireland gave Team Lotus their first Grande Epreuve victory with the much-improved and very sleek Lotus 21 spaceframe chassis car; for 1962 fast-developing Jimmy Clark became the Lotus number one driver, and Chapman devised a new car for him.

There had been constant problems with tubular chassis chafing and puncturing the aluminium fuel tanks strapped to them, and the Lotus design team was at this time developing a backbone girder chassis for a new road car–which eventually emerged as the Elan.

Tests showed this slender backbone to be immensely rigid, and Colin visualized widening it until there was room for a driver to sit between its side sections, and boxing in those side sections to create fuel tank space. Thus the epochal Lotus 25 was evolved, but it was a new idea and to hedge his bets Chapman also laid down a spaceframe alternative to pick up the latest all-independent suspension system developed for the Lotus 25.

The Lotus 25 chassis was formed in aluminium sheet, fitted over internal sheet bulkheads with not a tube in sight. It looked like an open bathtub in which the driver sat with fuel on each side of him. The new Coventry Climax FWMV V8 engine was behind his shoulders. The 63 mm × 60 mm engine had a displacement of 1494 cc, and produced about 190 bhp at 8500 rpm. Climax engines, incidentally, were now used by most British chassis-constructors, including Brabham, Cooper and Lola; only BRM, Porsche and Ferrari still made not only their own racing car chassis, but also the engines and transmissions.

The Lotus 25 made its debut in the 1962 Dutch Grand Prix and Clark led until suffering transmission troubles. He first won a Grande Epreuve in the car at Spa in Belgium, then won the British and United States Grands Prix. He led most of the way during the South African Grand Prix, but lost the World Championship when his engine lost its oil.

The Type 25 grew up into the wide-tyred 200-horsepower Lotus 33 as driven to victory here at Silverstone in 1965 by Jim Clark.

Jimmy Clark was virtually unbeatable during 1963 with the Lotus 25, the world's first successful monocoque-chassised Grand Prix car, originated as seen here in 1962.

During an incredible 1963 season, however, the Lotus 25 theme was developed and Jimmy Clark won a record seven of the year's ten Championship rounds to claim his and Lotus's first world titles. In non-Championship races, Clark and the 25 won five more events.

The Lotus 25 was the tap-root of modern racing car design and its immediate derivatives included the Indianapolis Lotus-Ford 29 and 38. These cars turned the Indy establishment away from the Offenhauser roadsters, reminiscent of 1939 Maseratis, towards the pure performance potential of road-racing-derived modern chassis.

In 1964 the much-improved, big-wheeled Type 33 was introduced by Lotus and with updated 25s saw Clark challenging hard for the Championship yet again, only losing it on the last lap of the last race–in Mexico City. In 1965 Clark took the Championship convincingly in his Lotus-Climax 33s, winning six races–five consecutively. He also won the Indy 500 in a Lotus-Ford 38 with 4.2-litre V8 engine.

As the Lotus 33s with two-litre engines continued racing in the first two seasons of the new three-litre Grand Prix Formula in 1966–67, so all constructors save Brabham followed the Lotus monocoque lead. Colin Chapman's innovation had succeeded in 1962 where Gabriel Voisin's had failed in 1923.

Jack Brabham drove his BT19 to victory in the French Grand Prix—and then on to the Drivers' World Championship. The engine was developed from an Oldsmobile original.

Repco-Brabham BT19
1966, Australia

Coventry Climax announced during 1964–65 that they would not be building a new engine for the three-litre Grand Prix Formula proposed for 1966. This move left such British specialist constructors as Lotus, Brabham and Cooper out on a limb. Lotus had Cosworth Engineering build them an engine with Ford money; Cooper turned to Maserati in Italy, who wheeled out a three-litre version of their age-old 2.5-litre V12 engine of 1957. Brabham looked to his native Australia and the Repco specialist performance equipment company there, who had helped fund his production racing car company upon its inception in 1961–62.

Repco took a very simple Oldsmobile F85 production V8 engine with an alloy block and developed it extensively for Formula 1 use. It offered a maximum 315bhp at 7250rpm from 88.9mm × 60.325mm cylinders, displacing 2995.7cc; there was a single overhead camshaft per bank. Installed in a very light and practical spaceframe chassis designed by Brabham's associate Ron Tauranac, this was to prove sufficient.

The chassis used originally had been laid down for a still-born flat-sixteen-cylinder 1.5-litre Climax engine in 1965, and it was quickly adapted to accept the new Repco engine. Running against H16 BRM, V12 Ferrari, V12 Eagle-Weslake, V12 Maserati and ultimately V8 Cosworth-Ford engines, this unit did amazingly well. Jack Brabham's BT19 won the 1966 French Grand Prix–the first to fall to a driver in a car bearing his own name–and then won the British, Dutch and German Grands Prix consecutively, clinching the World Championship titles for himself and for his cars.

In 1967 Ron Tauranac did 'a proper job' on the chassis, building the very compact BT24 car with which Denny Hulme won the Drivers' title, pipping his team-leader, who was content that his marque was for the second successive year Champion of the World.

Eagle-Weslake
1966, United States

Dan Gurney was an American enthusiast and a very talented Grand Prix driver. He won Grand Prix races for Porsche and Brabham-Climax in the 1.5-litre Formula of 1961–65 and then gained the backing to build his own Eagle cars for the new three-litre Grand Prix Formula of 1966 and for Indianapolis in America, in which race he had first interested Colin Chapman, and so brought about the Lotus-Ford rear-engined revolution there.

Dan and his backers established All American Racers Inc. at Santa Ana, California, late in 1965 and used Len Terry, designer of the Indy-winning Lotus 38, to draw his prototype Eagle cars for '66. Ties were then forged with Harry Weslake Research at Rye in England who were to build a BRM-like three-litre V12 engine for the Formula 1 variant of the Indy monocoque chassis. This wing of the company was named Anglo-American Racers and while development proceeded with the V12 engine Dan sorted out the first T2G Formula 1 Eagle chassis by using a 2.75-litre Climax FPF four-cylinder engine. He scored his first World Championship points for his own marque in the French Grand Prix that year, coming fifth, and was fifth again at Mexico City. The V12 Weslake engine was slow in arriving and proved a fretful baby, but in 1967 Dan became the first American driver in what was effectively an American car since Jimmy Murphy in 1921 to win a Grande Epreuve, when his Eagle-Weslake V12 won the Belgian GP.

Unfortunately niggling problems hit the V12s, and the Formula 1 activities of AAR faltered into 1969 and finally ceased. Dan's backers were primarily interested in US-style track events, and the Indy 500 in particular–which event an Eagle Offenhauser won in 1968; Eagle were to dominate that form of competition for many years.

Still, Daniel Sexton Gurney's heart was in road racing, and even today he remembers that Spa race with immense satisfaction.

Lotus 56B Turbine
1968, Great Britain

Peugeot, Delage, Mercédès and Ballot had done very well in the 500 Miles Indianapolis track classic in the World War I years, but European interest waned until the success of the Maserati 8CTF, influential in America. During the late forties and the fifties, Indy roadster design largely stagnated, the Miller-derived Offenhauser engine prevailing, although features such as disc brakes and fuel injection were adopted here earlier than in Formula 1.

In 1961 Jack Brabham finished ninth at Indy in a GP-derived 2.75-litre mid-engined Lotus Climax; in 1962 Dan Gurney drove a mid-engined Mickey Thompson car, and took Colin Chapman along; in 1963 the first Lotus-Ford Indy cars were placed second – and in 1964–5 the rear-engined revolution gripped US track racing.

In 1967, Andy Granatelli of the STP Corporation ran a gas-turbine-powered four-wheel-drive car at Indy and very nearly won the race. For the following year he hired Lotus to build a team of turbo-cars, and the dramatic wedge-shaped four-wheel-drive Type 56 was the result. The cars did not have a lot of power, but they handled supremely well. They were heading for an historic success when, with only nine laps of the 200 remaining both Art Pollard and leader Joe Leonard were side-lined by fuel-pump failure. Graham Hill's car had lost a wheel.

For 1969 the American track establishment reacted by effectively banning turbine power and eventually four-wheel drive, while spin-offs from the Lotus 56 programme included a flurry of unsuccessful four-wheel-drive Grand Prix cars and – in 1971 – an uncompetitive Type 56B gas-turbine Formula 1 car.

Matra MS11 V12
1968, France

In the early-sixties there was a tiny French specialist racing-car manufacturer named René Bonnet, which built monocoque Formula Junior cars after the Lotus fashion, but was very short of money. The mighty Matra aerospace company had a glass-fibre and plastics division which produced body panels for Bonnet's single-seater and long-distance sports-racing cars, and when Bonnet ran short of money, Matra's management absorbed his concern with the idea of promoting their engineering expertise through motor racing.

In 1964 a new one-litre Formula 2 for racing engines and one-litre Formula 3 for production-based engines came into effect. Matra built beautifully constructed monocoque single-seater cars for both classes, using British Cosworth-Ford engines. They proved very successful. In 1966 Ken Tyrrell, formerly Cooper Formula 2 team patron, was looking for a new chassis for the young driver he had brought to prominence in Formula 3 during 1964. That driver was Jackie Stewart. Ken was asked by Jean-Luc Lagardère, Matra's

dynamic young chief executive, to try one of the French chassis, and Stewart was instantly enthralled.

The Tyrrell Matra Formula 2 team raced very successfully through 1966–67, and in the latter season Ken saw the debut of the new Cosworth-Ford Formula 1 engine. He knew it might be offered to teams other than Lotus in 1968, and so managed to attract Stewart from BRM, and arranged for Matra to build chassis to accept the Cosworth-Ford engine; with sponsorship from the French ELF oil company he formed a Grand Prix team. In 1968 Stewart's Matra MS11-Ford won the Dutch, German and United States Grands Prix while Matra's own driver Jean-Pierre Beltoise handled the MS10 car with the Matra V12 engine installed. In 1969 a new MS80 car for Stewart proved outstanding with Ford power, and Jackie won six Grands Prix to clinch his first World Championship. Matra became World Champion constructor, and the object of their absorption of René Bonnet's failing little company five years previously was achieved.

◄ *Jackie Stewart driving his Anglo-French Matra-Cosworth to victory in the 1968 Dutch Grand Prix at Zandvoort on the North Sea coast.*

► *Jacky Ickx sliding his Ferrari 312B2 at Zandvoort during the 1971 Dutch Grand Prix.*

Ferrari 312B Flat 12
1970, Italy

Ferrari pulled themselves out of their 1955 trough by accepting the Lancia D50 gift; by 1959–60 their front-engined cars, though powerful, were old-fashioned, overweight and ill-handling compared to the rampant Britons. When the 1.5-litre Formula began, in 1961, Ferrari was the only team properly prepared with a really powerful multi-cylinder engine– a V6–and they won the Championships that year and also in 1964. For the new three-litre Formula in 1966 they developed one of their age-old sports-racing V12 engines to suit, and won races occasionally though in many cases unconvincingly into 1968. Then in 1969 their cars lost their competitive edge, and Ferrari fortunes slumped.

It was during this season that chief engineer Mauro Forghieri was developing with Franco Rocchi a new twelve-cylinder engine in which the cylinder banks were laid horizontally, opposing one another on a common crankcase. This flat-twelve engine placed its mass very low in the car, and thus potentially aided the car's cornering abilities; it was to develop into an extremely powerful unit,

which survived ten years in Formula 1.

The original 1.5-litre Ferrari flat-twelve had been developed by Forghieri for Formula 1 in 1964–65. A later development was the two-litre 212E engine which won the 1969 European Mountain Championship in a sports Ferrari chassis, and in 79 mm × 52.8 mm, 2998.5 cc form the unit made its three-litre Formula 1 debut in 1970 in South Africa. It was claimed to produce 460 bhp at 11,600 rpm but was thirsty for fuel. In that year's Austrian Grand Prix, Jacky Ickx gave the new 312B (three-litre twelve-cylinder 'Boxer') its first victory, with team-mate Clay Regazzoni second. In Italy Regazzoni won; in Canada Ickx led another 312B 1–2 finish and the result was the same in Mexico City. New 312B2 models were developed for 1971 with revised suspensions, but the 1970 model was outstandingly beautiful in mid-engined Grand Prix car terms and has gone into racing history as Ferrari's Grand Prix turning point.

Ferrari were to have a low time again–in 1973–but bounced back from 1974, winning three consecutive Championships in 1975–77, then another in 1979.

Lotus-Ford 72
1970–71, Great Britain

From 1968 to 1974 seven successive World Championship Grand Prix titles were won using the Ford-financed Cosworth DFV V8 three-litre engine. Ferrari took the Constructors' titles from 1975 to 1977 but in 1978 the ageing though still very competitive British engine won again. The compact and very practical DFV won more Grand Prix races, well over 100, than any other engine in the history of motor racing and in modified form added victories in the Le Mans 24-Hours sports car endurance race and in the superfast Indianapolis 500-Miles track classic.

Lotus were deeply involved with the inception of this engine. Late in 1965 Colin Chapman asked Keith Duckworth of Cosworth Engineering if he thought he could produce a Grand Prix power unit for the forthcoming three-litre Formula. Duckworth considered that he could, and that development and launching costs would approach £100,000. Chapman interested Ford of Britain in the idea, and with Ford's backing and

Ford lettering on the cam-boxes the DFV made its debut in the 1967 Dutch Grand Prix in the stern of a brand-new Lotus Type 49. This car was designed by Colin Chapman and Maurice Phillippe as a no-nonsense chassis which would not cause any development problems and so divert attention from the engine itself during its teething stage. In fact the chassis and engine proved themselves first time out in a fairy-tale debut at Zandvoort. Graham Hill started his car on pole position after setting fastest time in practice, and when Hill retired, team-mate Jimmy Clark then took over to lead to the finish, the cars setting fastest lap–and an entirely new performance standard–on the way.

The Lotus 49 went on to win 11 Grand Prix races and numerous minor Formula 1 events until it was replaced in 1970 by the Type 72 model, which itself created another Grand Prix design revolution. In the old 49 Chapman had created a monocoque forward cockpit nacelle which simply terminated in a vertical bulkhead behind the driver's shoulders. The DFV engine was designed to bolt directly to that bulkhead, and to carry the gearbox and

► *Emerson Fittipaldi during the 1973 Spanish Grand Prix, with the Lotus 72.*

◄ *The great Swedish driver Ronnie Peterson in the Lotus 72 during the 1975 French Grand Prix at Ricard-Castellet on the Mediterranean coast.*

rear suspension loads itself, without the aid of any extra chassis structure. This became a standard feature in other DFV-powered cars which appeared during 1968, notably Matra and McLaren.

Now, the Lotus 72 continued this theme – which in fact survives to this day – but its forward monocoque nacelle was a perfect wedge-shape intended to create the maximum down-force from wind effect at speed, and so literally push itself down onto the track surface. This shape had been developed by Lotus in their 1968 Indianapolis Type 56 turbine-powered four-wheel-drive cars. In the Formula 1 Type 72 it was allied with a very sophisticated suspension system, which replaced the hitherto virtually universal coil-spring and wishbone systems with torsion-bar springs front and rear, leaving the space between the suspension links on each side uncluttered and open to the airflow. Brakes were also mounted inboard at front and rear to eliminate heat-soak through the wheel rims into the tyres, and this helped to allow the fitting of very soft and sticky Firestone tyres which on other cars would normally have grown so hot as to melt.

The Lotus 72 was above all a carefully integrated design, and once teething troubles had been sorted out early in 1970 it progressed from strength to strength; it brought Jochen Rindt his World Championship title – unhappily posthumous, since he was killed in a practice accident at Monza. In 1971 a rebuilt Lotus team continued to campaign the Type 72 and in 1972 Emerson Fittipaldi dominated the Formula 1 season with it, winning the World Championship titles. In 1973 Lotus took the Constructors' Championship with the 72 while Jackie Stewart won the Drivers' crown in a Tyrrell. It was the first time since 1958 that the Championships had been split between two teams. Then in 1974 Ronnie Peterson won very different Grands Prix, at Monaco, Dijon and Monza on both very slow and very fast circuits, to prove the old 72's continuing competitiveness. But during 1975 Goodyear's tyre monopoly took effect and Lotus found the special tyres required for the 72 no longer available.

The car abruptly fell from favour, tyre requirements made what had been its great attributes now obsolete, and a truly great Grand Prix car faded into dignified retirement.

Tyrrell-Ford 006/2
1973, Great Britain

When Matra ceased allowing Ken Tyrrell to run Ford engines in their chassis in 1970, the English one-time timber-merchant bought chassis instead from the new March Engineering concern. Meanwhile he realized that to provide his driver Jackie Stewart with the very best machinery, he ought to attempt building his own car. To this end, and in utter secrecy, he contracted ex-Ferguson engineer Derek Gardner to build an experimental Formula 1 car to accept the DFV engine. The car was ready in September 1970 and Stewart shone with it in the Canadian and United States Grands Prix to assure the Tyrrell team of sponsorship for their brand-new cars in 1971.

During 1971 Stewart's incredible driving prowess brought Tyrrell victories in the Spanish, Monaco, French, British, German and Canadian Grands Prix, and team-mate Francois Cevert won the US event. Stewart was World Champion Driver for the second time, and Tyrrell-Cosworth became World Champion Constructor in their first full season of competition.

In 1972 Stewart was briefly laid low by an ulcer, and although he won the Argentine and French Grands Prix for Tyrrell the season was dominated by Fittipaldi's Lotuses. Stewart decided that 1973 was to be his last racing season before retirement, and Tyrrell built a new model, numbered Tyrrell 006/2. With this car, short and stubby, highly swerveable and designed as a machine from which only the very finest driver could extract the utmost, Stewart won its debut race at Silverstone, then added victories in the Belgian, Monaco, Dutch and German Grands Prix. With his success at Monte Carlo he equalled the late Jim Clark's record of 25 Grande Epreuve victories, and his Dutch and German victories added two more to set the all-time record of 27 World Championship-qualifying Grand Prix wins.

The Tyrrell 006/2 was driven by new Tyrrell team-members Jody Scheckter and Patrick Depailler in 1974 before joining the World's largest collection of classic racing cars at Donington Park, near Derby, England where it can be seen – occasionally in action – to this day.

McLaren-Ford M23
1976, Great Britain

Bruce McLaren began his Grand Prix career as a youthful team-mate to Jack Brabham in the Cooper team in 1959–60. When Brabham left, Bruce became Cooper's number one and stayed with them until 1965. Meanwhile he had established his own private racing team, first campaigning and latterly building his own Tasman Formula and sports-racing cars from an early start in 1964.

Come 1966 and the start of the three-litre Formula, Bruce built his own Grand Prix cars, and in 1968, when he adopted the Cosworth-Ford DFV engine, the papaya-coloured McLarens began to win Grand Prix races. Bruce was tragically killed while testing a sports car at Goodwood in 1970, but his team survived him and after a period in the doldrums came back to prominence at Indianapolis in 1971 with a startling wedge-shaped projectile based on the Lotus 72 aerodynamic form.

For 1973 a Formula 1 version of this McLaren M16 Indy car was constructed, known with Cosworth engine installed as the

1976 McLaren-Ford M23.

M23. With backing from Yardley Cosmetics McLaren had a good season, with Denny Hulme and Peter Revson winning several Grand Prix races. The M23 cars were repainted to display Marlboro tobacco company livery in 1974 when Emerson Fittipaldi joined the team, and he clinched the World Championship for McLaren with a string of consistent if generally uninspired race places to support a handful of outright wins.

The M23 continued in ever-modified form through 1975, and in 1976 James Hunt joined the Marlboro-McLaren team. Hunt had a torrid season in which he equalled Jim Clark's record of seven Grand Prix victories, was disqualified from two and reinstated in one, finally beating Niki Lauda and Ferrari to the world titles in the final round of the series, at Mount Fuji in Japan.

With two World Championships to its credit, the McLaren M23 joined the select ranks of classic Grand Prix cars. Some still raced as late as 1979 in national F1 events.

James Hunt had a superb run of hard-fought success during the 1976 season in his Marlboro-sponsored McLaren M23s. Here in the Italian Grand Prix at Monza he was 'regulated' out of contention by a dispute over the fuel the team was using, and although this was the third legal wrangle of a troubled season afflicting Hunt and the McLaren team they won through to steal the Championship titles in the final race of the season, at Mt Fuji, Japan.

Lotus-Ford 79
1978, Great Britain

Special aerodynamic aids had appeared in earnest in Grand Prix racing on the superfast Spa circuit in 1968, when Brabham and Ferrari appeared for the Belgian Grand Prix with little wings on struts above their engine bays, and with vanes on the nose to balance them out. The wings were set at such an angle that the airflow over them forced the car down onto the roadway. The effect was to increase tyre grip in cornering, braking and acceleration. Since this aerodynamic effect, which might add 250–400 lb to the apparent weight of the car at speed, was not actually extra mass to be accelerated, cornered and decelerated, it was virtually a something-for-nothing development. It certainly contributed mightily to rapidly increasing lap speeds. In 1969 wings had become so huge that they became unstable, and regulations were made to limit them severely. These basic limits survived with little alteration into the mid-seventies by which time wings on racing cars were vital components of the design.

In 1976 Lotus were in deep trouble, trying to find a successful replacement for the much-loved Type 72. Colin Chapman, aerodynamicist Peter Wright and ex-BRM engineer Tony Rudd studied the problems, and considered that use should be made of the air going underneath the car, as well as that which passed over it. They devised a car which effectively carried wings on each side of its centre section; the space beneath the 'wings' was open to the airstream at front and rear, but boxed in on the outside and closed off against the road there by a sliding skirt system.

This car, the Lotus 78, made its debut in 1977 and set new performance standards with staggering speed round corners. Mario Andretti, Lotus number one driver, said, 'It feels like it's painted on the road'. Mechanical troubles in mid-season with development Cosworth DFV engines cost Andretti and Lotus the World Championships, but in 1978 an improved car, now the Lotus 79, joined the 78; Andretti and team-mate Ronnie Peterson achieved total domination, chassis excellence giving the Cosworth-Ford engine another World Championship and beginning a new age–that of 'ground-effect' racing cars.

Renault RS10 Turbo
1979, France

During 1979 several strands of technical advance in Grand Prix racing interwove and created a season of remarkable interest. We had the Lotus 78/79 ground-effects aerodynamic form being developed beyond Lotus's own reach by the French Ligier team, by Brabham (using Alfa Romeo V12 engines) and by Frank Williams' long-unsuccessful team making the best use of Arab sponsorship money. We had Ferrari building the brutal-looking 312T4 model in which their very successful and powerful flat-twelve engine was mounted in a chassis which made perhaps better use of the air going over the body top than any had previously. Their broad flat-twelve engine obstructed airflow through the ground-effects side pods–a problem which did not afflict the Cosworth-Ford-powered brigade with their engine's narrow bottom end, and which Alfa Romeo engineers had side-stepped by sparing little expense to build a V12 engine in place of the flat-twelve which had been used in Formula 1 by Brabham since 1976.

Then we also saw Renault using the 1.5-litre supercharged option in the Formula 1 regulations, with a V6-cylinder engine boosted by an exhaust-driven turbo-supercharger. In this system a small impeller vane is introduced into the flow of exhaust gases, and a spindle couples it to another impeller which forces pressure air back into the induction side of the engine. This turbocharger arrangement had been used successfully at Indianapolis for many years, then in sports-car racing, and Renault had introduced it to Grand Prix competition in mid-1977. By mid-1979, with a ground-effects chassis to make best use of the 550 bhp available from their tiny engine, Renault were competitive and they won the French Grand Prix–Jean-Pierre Jabouille achieving this signal honour for Renault in their first Grande Epreuve success since Szisz's first-ever Grand Prix victory of 1906.

But it was the Patrick Head-designed Saudia-Williams '07 which set the ground-effects car standard for the year, carrying drivers Alan Jones and Clay Regazzoni to several victories–the Swiss in the twilight of an honourable career. The Williams was neat, practical, uncomplicated and efficient–a perfect foil to the pioneering sophistication of the Renault.

Study of the modern ground-effects Grand Prix car unclad: Saudia-Williams at Silverstone, 1979, showing the suction pods either side of the slender monocoque chassis nacelle.

The Major Successes

The list which follows lists the most important competition achievements of the cars described in the book, or of cars closely related to them.

The name of the driver is given in brackets after that of the event.

1898 Panhard 1st *Marseilles-Nice, Paris-Amsterdam (Charron), Course de Périgueux (Leys), Paris-Bordeaux (Chev. de Knyff)*
1902 Renault 1st *Paris-Vienna (Marcel Renault)*
1902 Mercédès 1st *1902 La Turbie hill-climb (Stead); 1903 Gordon Bennett Trophy (Jenatzy)*
1902 Napier 1st *1902 Gordon Bennett Trophy (Edge)*
1904 Richard-Brasier 1st *1904 Gordon Bennett Trophy (Théry)*
1905 Darracq 1st *Circuit des Ardennes, Vanderbilt Cup (Hémery)*
1906 Renault 1st *Grand Prix de l'ACF (Szisz)*
1908 Benz 1st *1908 St Petersburg-Moscow (Hémery); 1st 1910 American Grand Prize (Bruce-Brown)*
1908–09 Lion-Peugeot 1st *1908 Chari, Sicilian Cup (Giuppone); 1909 Catalan Cup, Sicilian Cup (Goux), Coupe de l'Auto (Giuppone)*
1910 Hispano-Suiza 1st *Coupe de l'Auto (Zuccarelli)*
1911 Bugatti 2nd *French Grand Prix (Friderich)*
1911 Delage 1st *Coupe de l'Auto (Bablot)*
1911 Fiat 1st *1911 French Grand Prix (Hémery), American Grand Prize (Bruce-Brown); 2nd 1912 Grand Prix de l'ACF (Wagner)*
1912 Peugeot 1st *Grand Prix de l'ACF (Boillot), 1913 Indianapolis '500' (Goux)*
1912 Sunbeam 1st *Coupe de l'Auto (Rigal)*
1913 Mercer 1st *1913 Elgin, San Antonio (De Palma); 1914 American Grand Prize (Pullen); 2nd 1913 Indianapolis '500' (Wishart)*
1914 Mercédès 1st *1914 Grand Prix de l'ACF (Lautenschlager); 1915 Indianapolis '500' (De Palma)*
1921 Ballot 2nd *Grand Prix de l'ACF (De Palma)*
1921 Duesenberg 1st *Grand Prix de l'ACF (Murphy)*
1923 Benz 4th–5th *Italian Grand Prix (Minoia, Horner)*
1923 Delage *Broke World Land Speed Record (Tgomas)*
1923 Fiat 1st *Italian Grand Prix (Salamano)*
1923 Sunbeam 1st *Grand Prix de L'ACF (Segrave)*
1923 Voisin 5th *Grand Prix de l'ACF (Lefebvre)*
1924 Alfa Romeo 1st *Grand Prix de l'ACF (Campari), Italian Grand Prix (Ascari)*
1924 Sunbeam 1st *San Sebastian Grand Prix (Segrave)*
1925 Delage 1st *Grand Prix de l'ACF (Benoist/Divo), San Sebastian Grand Prix (Divo)*
1926 Bugatti 1st *Grand Prix de l'ACF, Spanish Grand Prix (Goux), Italian Grand Prix ('Sabipa')*
1926/7 Delage 1st *1926 British Grand Prix (Wagner/Sénéchal); 1927 Grand Prix de l'ACF, Spanish Grand Prix, Italian Grand Prix, British Grand Prix (Benoist)*
1926 Mercédès 1st *German Grand Prix (Caracciola)*
1926 Miller 1st *Indianapolis '500' (Lockhart)*
1927 Fiat 1st *Milan Grand Prix (Bordino)*
1926–27 Talbot 1st *Brooklands JCC '200' (Segrave)*
1929 Maserati 1st *1930 Tripoli Grand Prix (Borzacchini), 1931, Rome Grand Prix (Ernesto Maserati)*
1931 Alfa Romeo 1st *Coppa Acerbo (Campari)*
1931 Bugatti 1st *Monaco Grand Prix, Czechoslovakian Grand Prix (Chiron), Grand Prix de l'ACF (Chiron/Varzi), Belgian Grand Prix ('Williams'/Conelli), Tunis Grand Prix (Varzi), Moroccan Grand Prix (Count Czaykowski)*
1932 Alfa Romeo 1st *Italian Grand Prix (Nuvolari/Campari), French Grand Prix, Coppa Ciano, Coppa Acerbo, (Nuvolari), German Grand Prix, Monza Grand Prix (Caracciola)*
1933 Napier-Railton 1st *1935 and 1937 BRDC '500's, Brooklands (Cobb)*

1934–37 Auto Union 1st *1934 German Grand Prix, Swiss Grand Prix, Czechoslovakian Grand Prix (Stuck), 1935, Tunis Grand Prix and Coppa Acerbo (Varzi), Italian Grand Prix (Stuck), Czechoslovakian Grand Prix (Rosemeyer), 1936 Eifelrennen, German Grand Prix, Coppa Acerbo, Swiss Grand Prix, Italian Grand Prix (Rosemeyer) Tripoli Grand Prix (Varzi), 1937 Eifelrennen, Vanderbilt Cup, Coppa Acerbo, Donington Grand Prix (Rosemeyer), Belgian Grand Prix (Hasse).*

1934–37 ERA 1st *1934 Nuffield Trophy; 1935 1500cc Eifelrennen, (Mays); 1935 1500cc Pescara, Berne, Masaryk (Seaman); 1936 Coupe Rainier Monaco, JCC International Trophy, Picardy GP (1500cc); 1937 Isle of Man (1500cc), London Grand Prix, Imperial Trophy; 1938 Coronation Trophy, London Grand Prix BRDC Road Race; 1939 1500cc Albi Grand Prix (B. Bira) among many others . . .*

1934–37 Mercedes-Benz 1st *1934 Eifelrennen (Brauchitsch), Coppa Acerbo, Spanish Grand Prix (Fagioli), Italian Grand Prix (Caracciola/Fagioli), 1935 Monaco Grand Prix, AVUSrennen, Penya Rhin Grand Prix (Fagioli), Tripoli Grand Prix, Eifelrennen, French Grand Prix, Belgian Grand Prix, Swiss Grand Prix, Spanish Grand Prix (Caracciola), 1936 Monaco Grand Prix, Tunis Grand Prix (Caracciola); 1937 Tripoli Grand Prix, AVUSrennen (Lang), German Grand Prix, Swiss Grand Prix, Italian Grand Prix, Czechoslovakian Grand Prix (Caracciola)*

1936 Alfa Romeo 1st *1936 Penya Rhin Grand Prix, Hungarian Grand Prix, Milan Grand Prix, Vanderbilt Cup; 1937 Milan Grand Prix (Nuvolari).*

1936–39 Maseratis 1st *1936 1500cc Eifelrennen, Milan Grand Prix, Coppa Ciano (Count Trossi); 1937 Naples, Lucca 1500cc (Trossi), Tripoli Voiturettes, Florence Grand Prix (Dreyfus), Targa Florio Voiturettes, Milan Grand Prix (Siena), San Remo Grand Prix (Varzi), Coppa Acerbo Voiturettes (Rocco); Masaryk Voiturettes (Villoresi); 1938 Tripoli Voiturettes (Taruffi), Targa Florio Voiturettes (Rocco), Prix de Berne (Hug), Modena (Cortese), Albi and Coppa Acerbo Voiturettes (Villoresi); 1939 Targa Florio Voiturettes (Villoresi), Naples Grand Prix, Picardy Grand Prix, Albi Grand Prix (Wakefield)*

1938 Auto Union 1st *Italian Grand Prix, Donington Grand Prix (Nuvolari)*

1938 Delahaye 1st *Pau Grand Prix (Dreyfus)*

1938 Mercedes-Benz 1st *French Grand Prix (Brauchitsch), German Grand Prix (Seaman), Coppa Ciano (Lang), Coppa Acerbo, Swiss Grand Prix (Caracciola)*

1939 Alfa Romeo 1st *Livorno, Milan Grand Prix (E. Villoresi), 1938 Livorno, Prix de Berne (Farina), Pescara (Biodetti), 1940 Tripoli Grand Prix (Farina).*

1939 Maserati 1st *Indianapolis '500' (Shaw), 1940 Indianapolis '500' (Shaw)*

1947–51 Alfa Romeo 1st *1947 Swiss Grand Prix, Belgian Grand Prix (Wimille), Nari Grand Prix (Varzi), Italian Grand Prix (Trossi); 1948 Swiss Grand Prix (Trossi), French Grand Prix, Italian Grand Prix, Monza Grand Prix (Wimille); 1950 San Remo Grand Prix, Monaco Grand Prix, Belgian Grand Prix, French Grand Prix, Pescara Grand Prix, GP des Nations (Fangio), British Grand Prix, Swiss Grand Prix, Bari Grand Prix, Italian Grand Prix, BRDC International Trophy (Farina); 1951 Swiss Grand Prix, Bari Grand Prix, Spanish Grand Prix (Fangio) French Grand Prix (Fangio/Fagioli), Belgian Grand Prix (Farina)*

1948–49 Lago-Talbot 1st *1949 Belgian Grand Prix (Rosier), Grand Prix de l'ACF (Chiron)*

1949 Ferrari 1st *Swiss Grand Prix, BRDC International Trophy, Italian Grand Prix (Ascari), Zandvoort Grand Prix (Villoresi)*

1950 BRM *No success at all in original form!*

1952–53 Cooper-Bristol 3rd *1952 British Grand Prix, 4th Belgian and Dutch Grands Prix (Hawthorn)*

1952–Ferrari 1st *1952 Swiss Grand Prix (Taruffi), Belgian, French, British, Dutch, Italian Grands Prix (Ascari), German Grand Prix; 1953 Argentine, Dutch, Belgian, British, Swiss Grands Prix (Ascari), French Grand Prix (Hawthorn), German Grand Prix (Farina) amongst others . . .*

1953 Maserati 1st *Italian Grand Prix (Fangio)*

1954–55 Mercedes-Benz 1st *1954 French, German, Swiss, Italian Grands Prix (Fangio); 1955 Argentine, Belgian, Dutch, Italian Grands Prix (Fangio), British Grand Prix (Moss)*

1955 Connaught 1st *Syracuse Grand Prix (Brooks)*

1955 Kurtis Kraft 1st *Indianapolis 500 (Vukovich)*

1956 Lancia-Ferrari 1st *Argentine Grand Prix (Fangio/Musso), Belgian and French Grands Prix (Collins), British and German Grands Prix (Fangio)*

1957 Maserati 1st *Argentine, Monaco, French, German Grands Prix (Fangio)*

1957–58 Vanwall 1st *1957 British Grand Prix (Moss/Brooks), Pescara and Italian Grand Prix 1957 (Moss); 1958 Dutch, Portuguese and Moroccan Grands Prix (Moss), Belgian and German Grands Prix (Brooks)*

1959–60 Cooper 1st *1959 Monaco, British Grands Prix (Brabham), Portuguese and Italian Grands Prix (Moss), United States Grand Prix (McLaren); 1960 Argentine Grand Prix (McLaren), Dutch, Belgian, French, British, and Portuguese Grands Prix (Brabham)*

1960–61 Porsche 2nd *1961 French, Italian and United States Grands Prix (Gurney)*

1962 Porsche 1st *1962 French Grand Prix (Gurney)*

1962–63 BRM 1st *1962 Dutch, German, Italian and South African Grands Prix (Hill); 1963 Monaco and United States Grands Prix (Hill)*

1962–65 Lotus 1st *1962 Belgian, British, United States Grands Prix (Clark); 1963 Belgian, Dutch, French, British, Italian, Mexican and South African Grand Prix (Clark); 1964 Dutch, Belgian, British Grands Prix (Clark); 1965 South African, Belgian, French, British, Dutch, German Grands Prix (Clark)*

1963 Lotus 29 2nd *Indianapolis '500' (Clark)*

1965 Lotus 38 1st *Indianapolis '500' (Clark)*

1966 Repco-Brabham 1st *French, British, Dutch and German Grands Prix (Brabham)*

1966–67 Eagle 1st *1967 Belgian Grand Prix, Race of Champions (Gurney)*

1969 Matra 1st *South African, Spanish, Dutch, French, British, Italian Grands Prix (Stewart)*

1970–71 Ferrari 1st *Austrian, Canadian and Mexican Grands Prix (Ickx) Italian Grand Prix (Regazzoni); 1971 South Africa and Questor Grands Prix (Andretti)*

1973 McLaren 1st *1973 British and Canadian Grands Prix (Revson), Swedish Grand Prix (Hulme); 1974 Argentine Grand Prix (Hulme), Brazilian, Belgian and Canadian Grands Prix (Fittipaldi); 1975 Argentine and British Grands Prix (Fittipaldi), Spanish Grand Prix (Mass); 1976 Spanish, French, German, Dutch, United States and Canadian Grands Prix (Hunt)*

1970–75 Lotus 1st *1970 Dutch, French, British, German Grands Prix (Rindt); 1972 Spanish, Belgian, British, Austrian Italian Grands Prix (Fittipaldi); 1973 Argentine, Brazilian, Spanish Grands Prix (Fittipaldi), French, Austrian, United States Grands Prix (Peterson); 1974 Monaco, French, Italian Grands Prix (Peterson)*

1973 Tyrrell 1st *BRDC International Trophy, Belgian, Monaco, Dutch and German Grands Prix (Stewart)*

1977–78 Lotus 1st *United States Grand Prix (West), Spanish, French, Italian Grands Prix (Andretti), Belgian Grand Prix (Nilsson); 1978 Argentine, Belgian, Spanish, French, German, Dutch Grands Prix (Andretti), South African, Austrian Grands Prix (Peterson)*

Index

Note: page numbers in *italics* refer to illustrations

ACKNOWLEDGEMENTS

Picture Research: Tim Auger and Elizabeth Rudoff

Photographs: Classic Car 72, 73; Gerry Cranham 8; Geoff Goddard 12, 27, 39 *(top right)*, 40, 48, 49 *(both)*, 51 *(bottom)*, 53 *(top)*, 71 *(top)*, 74, 79, 80, 81, 82, 83, 85, 87; London Art Technical 13 *(left)*, 77; Michelin 17; National Motor Museum 10, 11, 13 *(right)*, 16, 20, 21, 25, 28, 29 *(top right)*, 30, 31, *(both)*, 36, 37, 41, 50, 51 *(centre)*, 61 *(both)*, 67, 71 *(bottom)*; Nye 29 *(top left)*, 42, 57, 60, 75, 76; Cyril Posthumus 38, 39, 43, 53 *(bottom)*; cover